BETWEEN WORLDS
MY TRUE COMA STORY

WRITTEN BY
GERRY CULLEN

First Published in 2022 by Blossom Spring Publishing
Between Worlds: My True Coma Story © 2022 Gerry Cullen
ISBN 978-1-7398866-8-4
E: admin@blossomspringpublishing.com
W: www.blossomspringpublishing.com

FOR MY MUM AND DAD

WHAT WE DO IN LIFE ... ECHOES IN
ETERNITY
MATTHEW 9: 35-38

ACKNOWLEDGEMENTS

My sincere and heartfelt thanks to my Consultants at Leeds General Infirmary. Mr. David O'Regan for his truthfulness and encouragement about having open heart surgery. Doctor Wazir Baig for all the aftercare concerning my new Aorta valve.

Thanks to all the Surgeons who contributed to saving my life and giving me a second chance at Leeds General Infirmary.

Thanks to all the Doctors and Nurses in Intensive Care. (Ward 6)

Thanks to all the Doctors and Nurses in The High Dependency Ward. (Ward 16)

Thanks to the Doctors and Nurses at Pinderfields Hospital in Wakefield. (Cardiac care)

Thanks to the Doctors and Nurses at Dewsbury District Hospital.

My special thanks to Ronnie and Frank for all their inspiration and help in the Cardiac Ward at Pinderfields Hospital, Wakefield.

My incredibly special thanks to GOD for answering all my prayers giving me a second chance, for changing my life with the wonderful "Gift" out of my induced coma.

Thank you to Claire Voet and everyone at Blossom Spring Publishing for their arduous work and enthusiasm for this, my first book. Thank You, for choosing to read BETWEEN WORLDS: MY TRUE COMA STORY. I hope you find it inspiring and thought provoking.

Thanks, as always, to my beloved partner for everything.

TIMELINE: PAST, PRESENT AND FUTURE

After having major open-heart surgery at Leeds General Infirmary, in March 2018, I received "A Gift" out of my induced coma. I do not know why I received it, or where it came from. All I know is, that I was incredibly lucky to have received it. I look on it as a "blessing" in my life.

Was it inspired by my beliefs? I know that my life has changed for the better, because of it. I believe it to be, Heaven sent.

I had a "spiritual awakening" with pre-warnings through messages in dreams from April 2014. They lasted for over four years and seemed to inspire everything going forward. They were a comforting reminder of what was to happen in the future.

What follows is a true and real account of events, leading up to having major open-heart surgery at Leeds General Infirmary in March 2018, and what happened after it. My story is unique.

People who are in comas are "between Worlds" and their friends and family are in a sense "between Worlds" with them. They do not "crossover" because something in their World is not complete.

My true story continues today as do the messages. My writing is flourishing. I had never written books or for TV before. This is My Story.

REVELATIONS

GOD WORKS IN MYSTERIOUS WAYS
HIS WONDERS TO PERFORM

My name is Gerry. I am a practising Roman Catholic. My faith is important to me. I was baptized and confirmed by various Parish Priests in the Leeds diocese at St Mary of the Angels, Batley, my home parish.

I am of Irish descent. I am proud of my Yorkshire heritage and the fact that my roots go back three or more generations. My grandparents originated from Charlestown, County Mayo in Ireland.

I am from a large family. My Mum and Dad, Mary and Edward were wonderful. I adored them both. My Mum used to wear fine elegant clothes especially for do's and weddings. She used to buy her clothes in Leeds at a shop by Norman Hartnell. He was the dressmaker to the Queen. My Mum had a profound sense of humour. That is where I get mine from. She had four sisters and a brother.

My Dad, Edward, was not as tall as me; I am 6ft tall. He used to dress well, in a suit with a tie and shirt at weekends for mass. He had a wicked sense of humour too. They both moulded me into who I am today.

My Grandparents came to England by boat to Liverpool, during the potato famine in Ireland. They both died in the 1920s, sadly I never knew them, but I know we will all meet again. They and other Irish immigrants all built St Mary's.

My life began when I was born at Staincliffe Hospital in 1953.

The first 9–10 years of my life was living behind the

"Zion Chapel" in Batley. I lived there until 1964. We moved to another house near Batley Park in 1964 and I attended St Mary's RC school. It "was expected" in those days that all children would attend Sunday mass and be good practising Catholics.

I had a wonderful childhood. We had our difficulties, like most families, but it was a great time to grow up. Things changed in the Sixties and music and clothes were a major influence.

My Mum had a *gift*. She could read tea leaves, the coal fire and predict where someone was or find them. Somehow, I seem to have inherited that. Well, part of it. It is a form of *telepathy*. I can read *the signs* and I have received messages, prior to waking from sleep, in a dream. Is it my Guardian angel? Incredible I know, but it is all true. I do not know why I have been chosen and never will. Not in this World anyway.

Back in the '50s and '60s everyone on TV spoke the Queen's English and were polite. We only had three channels but had quality programmes to watch. School dinners were abysmal! They were dire and somehow, I can still *smell* them in the dinner room. On certain days we had cheese pie and were forced to eat it. No choice back then. I'm afraid that put me off cheese for life. It was a vastly different World. As there were few televisions in the '50s we made our own entertainment. We played cowboys and Indians, played conkers, built dens, played football, and re-enacted scenes from the latest film showing locally. Families would gather round the radio and listen to the latest music, drama or comedy shows. We all loved cartoons and had double bill showings at the cinema featuring the latest movies.

My first day at school was memorable—for all the wrong reasons. I remember a teacher giving me a nosebleed; my Mum really let them know about that one! Teachers and Nuns at that time were strict, woe betide if you stepped out of line. Back in those days we had to take punishment for doing wrong. I remember taking part in a Saint Patrick's Day school concert, I played a pirate in one show. I remember the lines I had to say to this day...

"I'm a pirate horrid and hard, I shot my aunt in her own back yard, Roderick Roper is my name, and you'd better not mess with my little game." Funny how you remember such things all these years later.

We also took part in Delaney's donkey doing all the actions to the song on stage and of course everyone was involved in McNamara's Band at the end. I was a child of the '50s but I grew up in the '60s. We all took our 11+ back then. Sadly, I didn't pass but I went on finding my way in life elsewhere. The Swinging Sixties were vastly different to the Fifties, although we did obtain our very first black and white television back then. We didn't get colour television until the late Sixties. Back in those days most of the television sets were rented from our local TV supplier.

In September 1965 I attended school at a Business College in Bradford. I was eleven-years-old. It had a massive influence on my life. I seemed to blossom there, yet I was very shy of girls. I put that down to the fact, that in the old days we used to have separate boys and girls playing areas. I do not really know the answer, but that is how it was back then. It was a real awakening in so many ways. I used to get teased by some girls, but I eventually blossomed. I had several crushes on some girls too.

I was at college until July 1971, and it was always a happy type of atmosphere, not like being at school at all. Teachers genuinely cared about all their students... there were no favourites. You felt as if you belonged.

Music played a significant part in all our lives, and we were hooked on Sixties songs and the era. I bought my first light blue and grey record player and collected lots of records.

I have dramatized part of this in my "Beyond Time" series, as you will see, later in this book.

Between Worlds - My story continues as follows...

A typical January day... 14th January 2018 to be precise. It is dull and grey but no snow and that is something to be thankful for. My beloved partner is reading her book and our cat "Angel Tom" is asleep on our bed.

Dreams are vivid and come and go but no message today.

I should explain that since April 2014 I have received messages in dreams... they continued for over four years. Why this has happened is not known, but they are real, and always spoken at the point of waking from sleep. I thought they were a *warning* at first but then I realised their meaning had inner depths and mean so much more. The dreams usually take place in a six to ten-month period and are usually of significant importance.

I am connected by way of telepathy... it is a one-way system. I have not found the way to communicate back. My connection is to Heaven. Daily messages on the radio (all stations) continue to flourish and I remember one which had a major influence, it was a hit in the summer of 1987.

My Mum died that year.

Her name was Mary.

The words were very poignant.

They gave me a feeling of hope and it influenced my life.

All of this happened after listening to a certain Christmas song while reminiscing. I knew the song, but it was always in the background and like most people, I never really knew all the words. I realised that in the words of this song was a communication. I cannot believe that I had been oblivious to that fact; it was as if my eyes had been opened for the first time. After hearing that song continually over Christmas, messages came in the words of other songs on the radio... up to forty a day at work.

Astonishingly, amazingly, I still have brown hair at sixty-four with a little grey. I put this down to my faith and Catholic upbringing and my staunch beliefs. My sideburns are still ok but more salt than pepper.

It is strange to think it is over fifty years since 1968 when I was fourteen. It was a vastly different World then.

The Swinging '60s, the permissive society and hippies, a World away from today's politically correctness, I am not a fan. It was so different in the '50s and '60s.

Somehow things were simple, yet everyone had time for one another. Neighbours were neighbours in those days, and it is true when they say, you could leave your door open, and no one would come in.

Life back then changed all over lives. I can recall all those lovely memories in my mind and relive them again, whatever that age may be. I am amazed just how incredible the human mind is and how it records and stores all this information. There is so much more to say and so many memories, but this book is not about me.

There would have been no book at all, had I not received those messages in dreams. When God calls, you don't say no.

Was I touched by the Hand of God?

I have never really explained how those messages affected me or how they changed my life.

I have barely touched on that. I felt it better to record them and then comment on their message later. I was not aware, just how significant, those messages would be.

My story begins, back in October 1987. My Mum had died in September and exactly three weeks later I had an extraordinary dream...

My Mum was in a garden, looking younger, sitting on a bench...

She said, "You think I'm gone, but I'm still here, and I'm still watching over you."

I remember it well, as she spoke to me just before waking from sleep, no doubt for maximum affect. I never had this dream again, or any other message, until something happened thirty years later; I began to experience messages all over again in April 2014.

I have somehow become a *reader*. It is a gift, heaven sent. Everything that is written is the truth. This is happening and continues to happen to me here, and now. I do not know why I was chosen or what those signs and messages mean. Do other people get messages like me?

They have intensified since I had a relapse in June 2015 reassuring me of a World to come. I was *touching heaven* that day, but it was not yet my time to leave this World.

APRIL 2014—My first message.

At the point of waking from sleep, a young man's soft voice saying... "Leave them to God."

I said to my partner, "someone has just spoken in a dream."

I told her what had been said. I asked if she had heard the voice, but unlike me, she had not heard it.

I thought it was a warning at first, not sure what it meant.

JAN 2015—Message 2.

Again, spoken by a young man's soft voice...

"The Book of Revelation."

This deals with the end of the World, and I have never read it. Angels are in the Book of Revelation.

REVELATION—To reveal, is to openly allow or see,

what is about to come. Am I about to see what is about to happen?

AUGUST 2015—Message 3.
Again, at the point of waking from sleep...
"The wood of the Cross"
It refers to a prayer which the priest says on Good Friday, at The Lords Passion. The full prayer is as follows...
Behold The Wood of The Cross
On which hung The Saviour of The World
Come Let us worship.

JULY 2016—Message 4.
Oh Clement
Oh Loving
Oh, Sweet Virgin Mary
A prayer that the priest says after five decades of the rosary.

APRIL 2017—Message 5.
I had a dream, where I saw someone wearing a long trench coat with long hair in front of me. When they turned around, I saw it was Jesus. Someone started to sing...
A popular song in the background.
It was another communication.

SEPTEMBER 2017—Message 6. In a dream...
A young girl and her mother saying, "Who do you think you are?"
A voice answers... "WONDERFUL COUNSELLOR... I AM

8

HIS MESSENGER"

I was intrigued with this message and decided to investigate on the internet. Why was it spoken at the end of September and not at the end of December? I found out the actual birth took place on 11–09–3BC. This would explain why the message was spoken in September.

All of this has happened in the last four years. It has changed my life. I feel sure that I am not the only one who knows this.

Like everyone else, I celebrate Christmas in December, and still do.

Friday 27th October 2017, early hours... I had a dream. My partner and I were standing at the bottom of a staircase. I said,

"Look up. Can you see the blue sky and clouds at the top?"

It was a beautiful day. We walked up the staircase. At the top was a lighted doorway. It was a brilliant white light. I looked in and could see other lights moving about. They were people. I asked,

"Why are you here?"

Someone said, "We are waiting."

"Waiting for whom?" I asked.

"Waiting for Jesus to come" they replied. I then awoke.

AUGUST 2018 (AFTER HAVING OPEN HEART SURGERY) in a dream just before waking, the following words were spoken by a young man...

"WHAT WOULD YOU DO IF GOD SPOKE TO YOU

THROUGH HIS MESSENGER?"

THE MESSAGES
(1) Leave them to God—May 2014

(2) The Book of Revelation—January 2015

(3) The Wood of the Cross—August 2015

(4) Oh Clement, Oh Loving, Oh sweet Virgin Mary—July 2016

(5) Another communication happened when I heard a popular song in the background—April 2017

(6) In a dream—An older woman (mother) and a young girl say, "Who do you think you are?"

A voice answers—"Wonderful Counsellor, I am His Messenger"— Sept 2017

(7) What would you do if God spoke to you through His Messenger?—Aug 2018

CHRISTMAS 2014

During Christmas, I received three *visual signs*. I am now able to read the signs. I had two on Christmas day.

The first involved three squirrels. We live on an estate where once stood a General Hospital. It was built in the 1920s. All the trees are under protection order by the council, and you require permission if they need cutting; this must be conducted by a professional tree surgeon. One of the squirrels left a nut on their box and then promptly came back to eat it. I likened this to the visitation of The Three Kings.

The second sign was by way of a *chink* in the curtains in our front room. It just happened to shine on a

Christmas card that depicted the child in the manger with Mary and Joseph.

The third sign came on Boxing Day when I saw a DVD in a supermarket. It seemed to link into my communications. Is someone trying to tell me something?

ANGEL SIGNS IN ITALY

After a day out in Skipton, we returned home late evening. A white cat with black markings came into our garden. He looked as though he had *angel wings* on his back. We called him and he came to us. He was unloved, had sores on his neck and back, dirty, and very hungry; we fed him seven saucers of milk. We had no cat food then.

He has never left us, and like all cats rules the roost now. He slept on an old towel, on a rock, in the back garden and was wet next day. At first, he slept outside in a box but then somehow found his way into our kitchen, like cats do... to be fed. He was getting his feet under the table.

He now looked much better. We started to treat his sores with antibiotic powder and are still doing so; they seem to flare up in the summer. Cats do not wash or clean themselves, if unfed or unloved. We never found a single flea on him. Someone must have dumped him, and to this day, he is afraid of bin liners and carrier bags, and the noise they make. Tom's sores were treated by the vet in liquid steroid form with tablets and expensive steroid needle injections. We love him though, and want the best for him, and not to be in any pain or discomfort.

After countless visits to the vet, he looks much better, and the various treatments seem to be working. We decided to call him "Tom" or "Angel Tom" as he is a big tomcat.

We were due to go on holiday to Italy in September and I had heard someone calling him. I advised my partner and thought it best to let him wander back to his possible owners.

July 2015. I decided to take a stroll around our local park, and then sat by the lake. I noticed that a man was putting a model yacht on the lake. I could not make out the word on the sail, but it seemed to read *Angel.* I took a photo on my mobile as evidence. It did say Angel—I was not dreaming, and I took this to be a sign. We thought Tom belonged to someone at the back, but we think they were just feeding him, he came back to us. We were so happy.

I do not know how these things happen, or who sends those messages, or why I receive them.

Tom now has a lovely home and is fed and loved. He is also happy and comfortable.

This is what happened while we were away...

Saturday 9th September 2015.

A large pet carrier at Cambridge Services. It had pawprints, and was on its way to Dover, for the crossing.

"Angel poster" an illuminated electric sign; in the foyer of our overnight Hotel, just outside Paris. Photo on mobile as evidence.

AT OUR HOLIDAY HOTEL, DIANO MARINA, ITALY.

Garfield with *angel wings* in glass cabinet in reception. It was a pendant. We had never seen Garfield with wings before.

SIGNPOST—"ANGOLO DI SOGNO" (also on phone)

We could see this from our balcony, at the front of the hotel. I thought *Sogno,* was Italian for song, but it means dream or dreams.

"ANGEL OF DREAMS" Very uncanny. Who is sending all these messages and why?

OUR RETURN HOTEL, REIMS, FRANCE.

Black and white cat on chair in reception.

Angel postcards in rack. Symbol of Reims Cathedral.

Tom has now been adopted. He is also an incredibly special cat. Is he the one, who can relay visual messages, who has telepathy, or do they come from a higher authority—and what is my role in all of this?

I am an ordinary man of a similar background, but I have incredible belief and faith. I think having this has helped me through my life. I have staunch Catholic beliefs, coming from an extraordinarily strong Catholic background and my heritage to County Mayo in Ireland.

What I do not have is religious mania. What I have is my life, which is deeply rooted in my beliefs. I do not know why I have been *given an insight* into things or what everything means. I hope it will all be revealed to me one day.

Back in the Seventies I used to write song lyrics. One comes to mind called... **MY LIFE IS MY SONG.**

Is there a meaning to this, and is it manifesting into what is to come, here and now?

HEAVEN IS HERE... NOW.

BACK IN THE DAY—RETRO—IT'S BEFORE MY TIME

Don't you just get fed up with hearing all these three lines?

Back in the day, it really was a wonderful time growing up. No hang ups whatsoever. I always used to say, "if it wasn't for back then, today wouldn't exist." Others look at it, as if you *belong on another planet* and yes, sometimes it feels exactly like that. Young ones today... "well they don't know they're born," to coin a phrase from an old TV ad. We hear the word *retro* all over the place today and we even sell *retro*. We too are retro. We lived through it all. What will they call it in fifty years' time? It feels like we are in a museum or time warp.

It really was a wonderful time in the '60s and '70s, but no matter what you say, you're somehow connected to the *retro* or *before my time* bracket.

Today so many things, appear to be clinical. There is no time for anything. Boy used to meet girl at dances and outside meetings. Today everything about dating is taking place on the internet or by speed dating. The pace is fast and ever changing.

I know good things happened *back in the day*. It might be *before your time,* but it all happened for real. I know it did, I was there. Even the moon landing in 1969 is under scrutiny today. We also now have trial by newspaper. *Back in the day*, no one would have been accountable, unless they had been convicted, by a Judge and jury. No one would ever have been named prior to that.

My, how times have changed.

A SIGN OF THE TIMES

More signs, continue to appear in songs and visually. If someone is wanting to get my attention, they have got it.

14th September 2016—Someone I knew had a tattoo which he showed to me...

It was a "FAITH ANGEL" on his right arm.

My partner had a similar dream to mine, when she also had a bereavement, and exactly three weeks later, she had the dream. She was informed "not to worry about him, he was well." My partner said he looked younger and was wearing a shirt with light slacks.

I had the same dream in 1987, when My Mum came to me.

This is about the closest we will get to Heaven, while we live our lives on Earth. If only someone could come back and tell us all about heaven. I have been given an insight, and it is a privilege to know what I have been given.

I am and never have been, worried about what is going to happen. No one can change what is about to happen, although, my human frailty got the better of me, the night before I had my operation. All of that will be revealed in the coming chapters.

My life belongs to God. (catechism) He alone will decide where and when, and at what time, it will end. He has the whole World in His hands.

More signs continue throughout September and October.

In June 2015 I had a TIA, also known as a transient

ischemic attack. It happened due to having a migraine. I spent over five hours at my local hospital being checked out. Nothing was found, at that time, concerning my heart. They had no idea what started it.

I do everything, in moderation now, no overdoing it. I spoke to two or three colleagues at work, they told me their partners had the same experience but had no reoccurrence ten years later.

A sign of the times is the World we live in today. 2016 is a completely different one compared to 1967 or 1973/1974. If I could choose, I would live back then when everything was different. Today, it feels as if we are trapped in some sort of time warp or black hole, and there is no way out. Yet everything is real. We must *make do* with what we have been given.

We all must accept *our cross* and carry on. We all have crosses in our lives, one way or another.

Our "Angel Tom" is different to other cats. I have already spoken of him, his abilities, and other things in earlier chapters. We have likened his various marks to angels' wings. He came into our lives for a purpose, although now, he is fast asleep on our settee. He lives the "life of riley." We keep saying we should have called him Riley.

The best things in life are free. This is true.

You give your time, your commitment, your help, your love... all for free.

You only get out of life what you put in... so make sure you live it to the full and enjoy it.

My story, is of course, not fiction. It is a true story, an

account of real events in my life. I never thought I would ever write anything about my life, but I am glad I decided to do it. I started by logging everything into a book in 2016, everything handwritten. I was worried that I would forget everything, up to that point, so writing it down helped, especially as I would need the information for this book. I have recorded dates, times of messages, as well as dreams and other matters which are all linked to my health condition. As it turns out, there is so much to say, so much to write about. I could never have just remembered everything, so many years down the line. It has all become part of my story, and it continues today. My main theme is my recent "communications." They are all true. I just could not make anything up like that if it were not real. I would not write or speak of it. I would not dare.

We are all destined to go on different roads, in our life. This is my journey. Have I received a "gift"? The answer to that question, may well lie in the future.

I somehow, feel compelled, to draft my story, although it is a little different, to what others may write about themselves.

My intention is to write a true account of my life, and that I, well, existed.

"What you see, is what you get," as the saying goes.

My renditions and facts are all true. We are who we are. Would I change my life and do things differently? The answer to that question is *yes* of course I would. Who wouldn't, given the choice?

You should be proud of what you have achieved in your lifetime, and quite rightly I am.

If my story, helps others, then I will be happy, no question about it.

Heaven... is it real? Does it exist? What do I have to do to get there? How do I get eternal life? These are questions we all ask. You only need to have "faith" to believe. There is no big secret. You must have faith. I am literally made up of generations of Catholic upbringing. It is in my blood.

To be "forewarned is to be forearmed." Does it give you more power to your elbow? I don't really know. All I know is to have "vision" helps to have clarity in our lives. More power to you if you believe in yourself. They used to call it positive thinking. The power of "prayer" is enough for me.

Visual signs and songs continue throughout December into 2017. I continued to draft three books throughout 2016 and into 2017. I also drafted a book based on music. It took me ten weeks to complete.

You know when you hear a certain song and it transports you back to where you were, who you were with? This is a book full of those memories.

It is incredibly special.

Here is just a snapshot of that time...

Back in 1967, it was a real awakening, for me musically, and in other ways too. I used to go to a place called "The Hole in the Wall" with two friends from college. It was just a doorway at the side of a coffee house in Bradford; you followed the stairs down into the basement. Tables and pinball machines were to the left. On the right was the "Hole in the Wall" that was all it was, but in there they played the most incredible music. It was frequented by "mods" and some "skinheads." Everyone drank a certain type of cola in bottles. No alcohol served in those days. We were all teenagers. All we cared about, was the music.

It was always played loud; when you came out your ears were ringing! It was a wonderful experience.

I only need to put on this music today, and I'm back at The Hole in the Wall. I was thirteen going on fourteen then. I remember wearing a shirt and tie with black trousers topped off with a brown imitation leather jacket. We all thought we were the "bees' knees" back then. We used to think we were all grown up. They used to have those fluorescent lights, on the walls of the disco; they showed up everything on your shirt, even tiny fragments on your clothes.

We had a FAB time though. We danced in our little group. No one bothered in those days. We were all there for the music—boys and girls together, everything was about the music. It was still an innocent time for me in 1967.

We were "off our heads" on '60s music. We didn't need anything else. Our lives were music, fashion, girls (even though we were afraid to speak to them) that's how it was then. We all loved the '60s, countless people still do today. I have always been a fan.

Summers seemed to go on forever, in those days. Wonderful memories of my time at college, and the now famous Hole in the Wall.

Years later, I wrote about it. My story came out of

"The Gift" in my coma. It was called "The Hole in the Wall." It was about my adventures there... this is how it began...

It's back to 1967 and the Swinging Sixties for this six-part comedy drama.

College friends Steve and Gerry discover "coming of age" through the magic of '60s music at the legendary Continental Coffee Bar in Bradford.

The Hole in the Wall is where all the action takes place... and it's where everyone wants to be. It's a time when Mod mania reigns supreme. Mini skirted girls are everywhere... but growing up is never easy in a World of innocence... even though this is the permissive society and flower power.

Eventually Steve and Gerry progress to the Bradford Locarno... where more adventures lie ahead.

THIS IS MY WORLD TODAY.

It had its own Soundtrack which was full of Soul and Sixties hits of the day.

We began to have nights out, at the Bradford Mecca Locarno. We started out at the teenager's disco on Tuesday evenings, then eventually progressed to Friday and Saturday nights. They had a records section and a live band. This is how it was for years. It had a shiny contemporary dance floor, which was quite huge. They played lots of Sixties records. You could lose yourself on that dance floor. The changeover used to take place in between records and the band. As it was the teenage disco, we had to leave before 9:30 p.m. It was college next day. Wonderful times.

Back in the Seventies, it really was the height of

sophistication. We used to go to Peter Stringfellow's "Cinderella's" in Leeds. You had to dress appropriately in those days. We would go to various boutiques and get the latest gear to look the part; we topped it off with all kinds of aftershave... it was as if we bathed in it really. Everything was all part of the time, the era. I used to wear 24-inch bell bottom, powder blue trousers, and a smart checked jacket complete with "poke your eyes out" collared shirts. We looked the part... and the business. It was how it was done in the Seventies. Girls wore miniskirts or hot pants, and they all seemed to have trendy hairstyles to match. Of course, everything changed when a certain movie came out, with the fabulous disco music.

After my life changing operation this prompted me to write another series which also came out of the "Gift" in my coma. I decided to call it... "DISCOTHEQUE."

"DISCOTHEQUE"— This is the story outline...

It's back to the '70s and '80s for this six-part comedy drama set against the backdrop of disco music and the ever-changing styles of fashion... in a very modern World.

Steve and Gerry recall their story, having frequent meetings at a Leeds Hotel, rediscovering a vastly different scene to that of the Swinging Sixties in all the disco venues of the day in Leeds and Bradford. Stylish and sophisticated... Girls have changed... they know what they want... and how to get it. Fabulous boutiques... 24-inch flares... hot pants... kipper ties... platform shoes... it's all here.

When Steve goes off to University Gerry must find his

own way in this real-life disco story... but when it all eventually comes together, everything takes off in a big way in the late eighties.

It all goes full circle when Gerry decides to hold a party in celebration. The Event/2020 Reunion is arranged. We invite old school friends and work colleagues to attend... also staff of Leeds General Infirmary... with Steve and Gerry as guests of honour.

GOOD TIMES ARE GUARANTEED.

Whilst the ability to "read" the signs has been handed down to me, I was never aware of just how influential they would become in my life. Yes, I can *read* the signs. I can also receive angelic messages. The songs on the radio can also speak volumes. I am aware that only I can see this. Other people may not have "The Gift."

Just what all this means is a mystery... or is it?

There must be a reason for all this. I intend to find out.

REASSURANCE

There is no mystery, everything is a reassurance of a World to come. Am I being prepared for what is to come? Does this happen to other people, and how do they cope with it? Is it part of "an insight" due to my faith and beliefs? It's not a big issue for me. I accept it for what it is. If I am being guided by fate, or being moulded, it may be for a reason. If I were to read between the lines, it is for my own good. I am sure all will be revealed in time. Patience is a virtue. I have been blessed, in many ways.

My first visit to Lourdes, in the South of France in 1988 may explain something. I had an "overwhelming experience" at the Grotto of Massabielle. I was standing near the River Gave de Pau when I suddenly felt a "power surge" against my body. It bumped into me; it was radiating from the Grotto. So many people have been cured there due to the "healing water." I can't explain why this happened.

Monday, 6th March 2017.

A very strange thing appeared in the sky tonight. It was a very bright star. It looked like an angel *hovering* with a tail. Was it real?

It was not a star. I do not know what it was. Are stars really Angels watching over us all? It was a mystery. Was it another reassuring sign? It seemed to be accompanied with *strange music* playing outside.

What does it mean, and where did it come from? Am I being guided home? Is it a sign from Heaven? I should have taken a video on my phone, to prove it was real.

We live in a World where you must have evidence and proof of everything. To simply say "I saw it" is not enough. Like "doubting Thomas" they must see everything, and would even then dispute that, one way or another.

Is someone trying to tell me something? I can "read the signs" but I am not sure what this one is saying. It is best not to go into too much detail. If this occurs again, I will get video evidence. Whatever it was, it is *revealing* itself to us.

More signs in song titles continue throughout February and March.

What is their message? Real... unreal... what is real? Everything, to me. It goes without question, there is no mystery if you keep the faith. There is a deep faith within me.

I have no regrets. I do not know what lies ahead, or which path I will take. I have a "guiding light" in front of me. What happened to me, has made my life less ordinary. Why have things been given to me, revealed to me? Everything means something. I am the same as everyone else, except I have opened my heart, and received a great gift. There is no trickery, no lies or anything else for that matter. I am who I am, that is what counts.

As for the future, no one can predict what will happen. I don't have the foresight to see into the future. Am I being prepared for something, and is this part of it? "Reading" or understanding the messages is also part of what I am going through.

This has become a daily occurrence for me. Others

may look upon it, as "a blessing." I do not know why this happens. It is a kind of *phenomenon*. Whatever is going on, it is happening personally to me. Not everyone would understand what it all means.

I think, looking back, there are things that occur in our lives, unexplained things, they happen for a reason. Whatever is going on it's very satisfying and deeply spiritual. Somehow things have become less ordinary. Something wonderful has been given to me, you cannot see it; you cannot feel it... you just know it is there. Is it intuition, as in a "sixth sense"? It may have always been there. Now unlocked. Is it in all of us?

I had another dream on 2nd April 2017. Usually, I can only remember tiny fragments. This time I could *visually* read the signs...

I remember a plane coming into land at Leeds-Bradford airport. I was waiting to get on it. It had no ordinary wings. It was as if it had wings like a bird or adjustment type ones. An Angel also has that type of wings.

I met a lady to discuss my books. She was incredibly positive and encouraged me to develop my story. I also remembered one of the messages... THE BOOK OF REVELATION.

This could refer to a Biblical message or to the books I am writing.

These may all be significant to my story.

Where I live, there seems to be significant "comings and goings" through our lights. This happens and is mostly noticeable on Autumn and Winter evenings. It is the site of a former General Hospital.

I am talking about "phenomenon" that go through our lights. They seem strong, when passing through, others are not.

What does it all mean?

Are they poor lost souls, who did not walk "into the light" when they died? Are they forever stuck here in Limbo? Did they also refuse to accept, that they were dead?

If they want to get my attention, they have succeeded.

How can I help them?

Do they know I can *read* the signs and want me to help them? It all means something, but I am not sure exactly what.

Easter Sunday, 6th **April 2017.** Another message in a dream...

It was sung in the words of a certain Seventies song. I remember the song becoming a number one and a massive hit in the Seventies.

The dream I remember, saw me crossing a marketplace going towards a Town Hall. I remember seeing *what seemed to be* a lady in front of me, with long dark hair, wearing a trench type overcoat. They looked round. I then saw that it was Jesus.

What if it was not the marketplace, but the road out of Gethsemane?

What is the meaning of all these messages?

Am I being prepared for what is to come?

It's wonderful to have received a message like this on Easter day. This has never happened before. It has been a year since the last one. My life is richer for having received them. Who knows what will happen in the coming months, or years that lie ahead? Things happen for a reason and a meaning. No one knows, what will happen in the future.

You must create your own luck. Channel your own talents into something you believe in.

Everything is a revelation to me. Is this what it means in the words "The Book of Revelation" although it could have meant something else at the time.

I may find out one day.

Will my journey eventually reveal everything?

Who knows what that may be?

I am sure that it will all become clear in the future.

Ask, and it shall be given you... seek and you shall find... knock and the door will be opened to you. LUKE 11:9

UNBELIEVABLE BUT TRUE

I remember driving home from work on Wednesday, 2nd May 2017 when a strange occurrence happened.

It was about 4:30 p.m. and for no obvious reason, the car heating came on. It had been set on to the "Lo" setting. I tried to turn it off, but instead it kept coming back on for a minute or so.

What does it mean? Was someone trying to contact me? Lo, was someone trying to say "hello"?

It was all very strange.

There is no human explanation that comes to mind when that happens. All you can do is accept it. If only they could predict the winning lottery numbers.

I heard a new song on the radio at work today. It gave me an idea to write a book about the times I spent in Leeds at a Singles Club in the late Eighties. I hope that I can write something soon. Now, every time the song plays it is like "an omen" to get motivated. Something for the future?

Signs in songs on the radio continue throughout April and May.

These songs are a constant daily reminder of just what is happening. There is no sequence. I only listen to them at work. There is no pattern or reason or answer why all of this happens.

It may have always been there, I just did not notice it in the past?

Nothing is ever easy in Life. We all must work hard to get things done these days, and I am no exception. You must believe in yourself, and put over your thoughts, as best you can.

I am amazed how my life has changed. I never wrote anything before "my coma." I just would not have known where to start with regards writing for film or television. It just was not there before.

Whatever happened to me, it really is amazing! I am so happy to have written several books about my life. It has not been easy, believe me, but now they have been written, they are an achievement on my part. Who knows where they will take me?

Everything I have written is real. Nothing has been mapped out at all. Just as in life, nothing is certain, nothing is set in stone.

We are dealt the cards we are given.

We must adapt, put ourselves forward, present ourselves in the best conceivable way. No one will judge your motives. Accept your fate, allow it to be changed.

What follows is a true account of my story. You may find it thought provoking.

I am advised it is, inspiring, extraordinary, and incredible.

What has been given to me is real.

"The Gift" continues today.

JANUARY 16TH 2018

It's a typical cold Winter's Day. Freaky weather conditions on my way home from work in West Yorkshire. We are not prepared for snow in this country unlike Sweden. We always get caught out with just a sprinkling. It's chaos on the roads; cars and trucks are all over the place, slipping and sliding.

I manage to get half-way up a hill but must turn back. Brave indeed.

I just kept saying "Oh God please help me" as I made my way down the hill, luckily in one piece.

Thank you for hearing my prayer.

I manage to drive into a supermarket carpark, thinking that I would have to leave my car there, but the conditions seemed to get better, so I decided I would try to get home another way.

I managed to get to the local Crematorium (hoping this was not an omen) but conditions became so bad I had to abandon my car. The traffic was grid locked, and so was all the town. I walked about a mile home and after stopping for breath, reached home eventually after 7:30 p.m. I knew something was wrong, something was happening to me. It is now over three hours since I left work. I still have problems with my chest and breathing, it feels like asthma gasping for two or three days. I had been to see my doctor at my local surgery, and he checked everything, but did not prescribe any antibiotics. He just gave me a leaflet and told me to return in three weeks if things persisted.

I have developed asthma again; I had it as a child, and

it persisted into my teens. The attacks were usually late at night, just before bedtime, and they left me gasping for breath.

It's now over two weeks since the freak snow fall, and I am assuming my condition is down to stress at work. I have been a Credit Controller for over thirty-three years, starting my working life in July 1971 and that's forty-seven years to date. Time has taken its toll though, I am now sixty-four, the pressure to perform is as challenging as ever.

It is not easy trying to obtain a Million (£1M) a month from customers. I was advised to "use charm." I applied that logic to my job at various companies and it always worked.

I had good teachers, Cyril, and Stanley, at Head Office in Manchester. One of the number of companies I worked for during my extensive career.

It's fair to say that it is a different World today. I have kept the "charming" method and it always worked for me. I was advised to "build relationships" with customers and Cyril used to tell me to ring and talk about something else saying "they will respect you and always pay."

He was right. Cyril recommended that I use my dulcet tones to obtain my goal and "charm" them and to never be vain or controlling. Right again. Cyril was a lovely man and I miss him. He also used to say, "it's one thing to have knowledge and another thing to have wisdom" and "God works in mysterious ways His wonders to perform."

It is a million miles away from how I started in 1985 to 2018.

Today my job is stressful and carries more

responsibility. Everything is scrutinised in microscopic detail. That is the way it is today. Every word is logged on to the electronic god aka the computer. They would not know where to start today without it.

Remember when we had phone boxes? (Red ones in the UK) They were everywhere and home telephones?

It was another time... another World... yet not so long ago.

Today's fast electronic World has no time for memories and if I hear anyone else say "back in your day"—you would think we were all Neanderthal's!

I am on a journey, childlike optimism, trust, and innocence shine through. There is a "guiding light"— destiny, a fresh start and excitement and a leap into the future. Mystery and a dash of genius, adventure, and a brilliant opportunity to remake my life. I have courage to see it through and where it will take me.

What has happened to me is nothing short of remarkable. My Mum used to take me to see Palm Readers when I was young. Being of Irish descent I am fascinated with finding out what Clairvoyants or Palm Readers have to say, and it's never changed. My Grandparents originated from Charlestown in County Mayo. After they died my Mum became the head of the Cairns family and assumed their role looking after her four sisters and brother in Batley, West Yorkshire. It is my hometown and the place of my birth. Like everyone else in the World, I am proud of where I come from, and my Yorkshire heritage.

I am a true Yorkshireman born and bred.

I am not superhuman, I am the same person I ever

was, but things have changed, I am a totally different person.

My journey, childlike or otherwise, is going forward and I await the next message or sign with anticipation and excitement.

I have had my palm read and had Tarot card readings on two occasions. I like to know about the future... my future. Predictions of good fortune in my life with my books have been foretold by the clairvoyant during the readings.

The freaky weather conditions of 16th January 2018, when I had to walk home, have left me with a bad chest and asthmatic breathing conditions. I manage to soldier on at work, but on Friday 2nd February, the pain became too much and affected my breathing. Certain individuals would misinterpret this as something else, but this is not the case.

My recent appointment with my doctor revealed my blood pressure, temperature and sounding of chest were normal but it is worrying. I have had time off work, to allow the bad chest condition to improve, and it has slowly done so thanks to a certain cough mixture.

"We can't give you anything" is the response from the Doctor so off I go with leaflet in hand hoping I will get better soon.

Three days later my bad chest has only slightly improved, and I managed to return to work on Wednesday, 7th February 2018. A colleague was talking about when he had the Aussie flu, and the symptoms were like mine. Was that the solution I was looking for?

He was gasping to climb the stairs. This was exactly what I was going through. My colleague told me he had to go to A&E (Accident and Emergency) where they gave him strong antibiotics to clear it. I had another relapse attack that evening when I could not catch my breath. It was another night without sleep. I was unable to go into work again.

I have worked for fifty years full time; this is the first occasion I have had to be away from work for so long due to illness.

I managed to get another Doctor's appointment on 8th February. The prognosis was that it was a nasty virus, and I too needed antibiotics to clear it. Doctors do not give these out unless it is necessary.

I received an extraordinarily strong seven-day course of 500mg per tablet. I had taken only two tablets, but they were already being effective. My breathing seemed to be slowly returning to normal, but I still had twenty-one capsules to take… nineteen more to go.

I decide to take two or three more days off work.

I am now under Doctor's orders.

THE DAY MY LIFE CHANGED
FRIDAY 16th February 2018

My life changed on this day.

I was still suffering from shortness of breath, and I had booked to see my doctor late afternoon at the surgery.

There is no need to search for answers anymore... the answer is me. I didn't realise it at the time but the messages I previously received in dreams, were obviously sent to reassure me of another World to come, and to give me guidance for what was about to unfold.

I could not have dreamed of what was about to happen to me personally, physically, and spiritually.

My doctor at my local surgery said I needed to go to A&E at my local hospital and he printed off all my notes. The Doctor recommended that I park my car, next to the surgery, and take a taxi at once up to the hospital. I followed his instructions without question. The taxi came and I arrived at A&E within ten minutes. I was still gasping for breath.

Five hours later, after a series of tests in the hospital, I transferred to another regional hospital. I remember, the doctor on duty, was not pleased at all that I had arrived by taxi and said I should have arrived by ambulance from the surgery.

I had a dream prior to going to see my doctor after dozing off in the afternoon.

The dream was in a "vision." I saw myself alive and well in the future.

I was in Resus, A&E and Cardiology also known as the Cardiac Ward. I have never had a heart-attack, nor do I want one.

The positives were that I had never smoked, and only had the odd glass of wine, on a rare occasion, which helped tremendously with my assessment.

The eventual diagnosis was that I had a "heart murmur/irregular heartbeat." It was something I could have had from birth, without knowing it. Although I do remember, the odd skipping a beat, and sudden racing heart, but like all normal people, I never put it down to anything, and my doctor did not notice it in all those yearly MOT's.

My sister told me about my Mum waiting for a replacement valve, but it never happened, as it was unheard of, in those days.

Technology has advanced all of that today, 2018 is now in the realms of science fiction when it comes to operations and procedures in modern hospitals. I now realised that my irregular heartbeat/heart murmur could be hereditary.

I am now on a Cardiac ward. When I arrived in Hospital my breathing was erratic, and I could not go to sleep or lie on the bed due to the continuing problem. The nurses advised there was fluid on my lung's, and this was initially causing my shortness of breath in a big way.

I was unable to climb the stairs at home without being out of breath.

My cough mixture was never going to cure this.

Waiting to find out what will happen next, is the worst thing.

My doctors confirmed that I needed to have two teeth removed. I was not happy about this, but if it had not taken place inhouse by the Dentist the next stage of my operation could not be performed. It's something to do with the age of the teeth that does this. It may be the price I have to pay, to solve my breathing problems.

Eventually all breathing problems returned to normal. The fluid on my lungs had to be drained away in bottles before anything else.

They did it gradually.

"You'll pee for England" advised a Nurse and she was right. They asked me to use bottles, so they could measure it. All the Nurses were *angels* I cannot fault them. They had so much patience.

Ronnie (seventy-seven) and Frank (eighty-two) were major influences on the ward, they were so brave. I was so frightened—no doubt my human trait. They were so positive, so inspiring, they helped me settle in.

The little boy in me had returned. I had my appendix removed at Bradford Royal when I was twelve. It is the unknown, that fuels our fears. It is not the norm, and we, well I, simply did not know what was coming. Fears to one side, Ronnie had just undergone valve replacement and he showed me how to sit up to help. He was right poise is everything, and I thank him for all this. Frank was also an inspiration at eighty-two "I'm dying" he used to say. I was in admiration of them both, as I needed guidance. I was still gasping for breath, and it took time to drain the fluid from my lungs and get back to normality, but slowly and surely it happened. I would just get into bed, only to get out again, trying to catch my breath. As I say I eventually managed to get it back, but it was a slow process.

There were so many different characters on the Ward. Sadly, Colin had been there for months, one night he got up and said, "anyone for milk lads?"

I advised "Colin, we're all in hospital" He used to sleep day and night.

Weeks later, Colin died, of multiple organ failure. We were all so sorry.

The "Crash Team" were in action on dubious occasions, no matter what time, day, or night, saving lives and they did countless times. It was frightening.

Frank said, "it's the weekend, watch out to see what happens." We did not have long to wait. Two new arrivals came in. Just across the Ward, they brought in someone who was obviously an alcoholic. All he wanted to do was escape out of the Ward. He wanted his "cans and ciggies" and said he had not eaten for three weeks. Incredibly sad, but just how can you help someone, who does not want help? His daughters turned up next day and demanded he pay "another £60" that he owed.

It was very embarrassing for all of us in the Ward... then the wife rang. He told her where to go and said he would pay the next day. I guess he would drink that money away too.

We all had a very restless night. You cannot really sleep in hospital. This man wanted to go, and he tried every trick in the book to get away. He put his shoes on and began his run, only to end up with a fall against a wall. Security detained him. He still managed to discharge himself the next day. No one was sad to see him go.

Various characters, arrived on the ward, while I was in

there. It was a bit of a revelation I can tell you. The nurses all dealt with it professionally and nothing was too much trouble.

I am a light sleeper, so the lights left on all night and various snorers did nothing for my wellbeing or sleep. In the afternoons in the TV room, I used to watch reruns of The Persuaders. I had no idea how that would become part of my coma. I had to accept that all of this, was beyond my control, I had to take it on the chin as it was all part of what happens in hospital.

The Hospital is a massive complex. Its foyer resembled that of an airport terminal. I used to walk down the Ward to sit overlooking it next to the Nurses station.

I often visited the Chapel and prayed, it was beautiful and inspiring.

Mobile phone reception was extremely poor, all calls and texts were relayed back inside; I felt cut off from the World.

There were also two nasty characters on the wards. In the TV room, one of the patients monopolised it and I often made my way to my room or bed. Selfish people eventually left. I lost my voice, due to the inhouse heating system, which could not be switched off. Two patients were noisy, and I remember being informed by the Ward Sister if a room came up on its own would I be interested? Yes, was my answer. I would jump at the chance. Later that day a room became free, and I was glad to move.

ASSESSMENT

I am now in my new single room surroundings. It is heaven. No more snorers or loud talking patients. I am still awaiting a date, for moving to Sheffield or Leeds for my operation.

My sister and partner came to see me. For those who have been in hospital, boredom and looking at four walls is not fun. I dealt with it the best way I could.

I have said all along I am not a reader or writer at all. I had read all the newspapers and magazines that my sister brought in for me. I would look out of the window, as well as having my twice daily walks down the corridors, to the Chapel. It was my solace in hospital.

Meals were not particularly appetising. After two or three days everything tasted the same. The only redeeming quality, was the jacket potato and tuna coleslaw mix, or the salad plateau consisting of chicken, corned beef, or turkey. They were my staple diet in Winter.

The wintry weather outside, had now turned into "the beast from the East" with so much snow everywhere. The Hospital had their own snow ploughs, and they used them quite often to clear the roads. I would never have made it to work, the weather was so bad and dangerous.

A couple of my dodgy teeth were now due to be removed by the Dentist.

Various Doctors, always seemed to ask the same question "Did you know that you had an irregular heartbeat or heart murmur?"

"No" is my reply "I never knew it." They asked again

"Do you know you have low blood pressure?"

"No" is my response "I'm being treated, for high blood pressure by my doctor." The Doctor seem to be surprised by my response. My Dad had low blood pressure, but I had not. The Doctor said that I could have had it from birth, without knowing it.

I never knew that I had it at all.

My heart used to skip a beat, now and again, but I put it down to the heart and nothing more.

"You'll have to go for an angiogram, and we'll check on its condition."

"We'll let you know the day and time."

"We need this information before we can send you to Leeds or Sheffield, for your operation."

After waiting for two or three days, a nurse informed me that my angiogram was due that morning. I was like a little boy again, afraid of what it all entailed.

A Hospital Porter took me from my room in a wheelchair to the Angiogram theatre. I entered the room and the nursing staff assured me that it was normal procedure. An assuring pleasing pop song was playing in the background.

There were massive screens on the wall and cameras that came right into your face to record everything, from every angle.

"Don't worry" advises the Doctor and his assistants "you are safe, and it will all be over soon."

"OK we need to insert a micro camera; don't worry you shouldn't feel anything."

The tiny camera was on a chord type line. It was inserted into my groin. They were right I never felt a thing. It was amazing and it recorded everything. I could see it projected on the massive screen. It was a computerised recording. The other cameras that came so close to my face did the same. It was all over in half an hour. I returned to my room in the Cardiac Ward awaiting my results.

My first procedure was complete, followed by the next, being the extraction of two teeth.

The Doctors did their rounds every day assessing each patient.

Eventually a doctor confirmed that I was on the Leeds General Infirmary list, but it may be a while before I could arrive there.

The Doctors recommended that I did not leave hospital, as I would be moved down the list for procedure if I had gone home. I took their advice. I knew I needed the operation, and I had to wait. I did what the Doctor's told me.

The Doctors updated me every day and even Junior Doctors came and assessed me. They sounded my chest and took my pulse over and over. It was very tiring.

Eventually both Ronnie and Frank left, and a new batch of patients arrived. I was so glad to be in a room on my own, as someone who had just arrived was causing quite a stir, and every other word was bad language, I could hear them. It was appalling.

There is no need for such language in hospital and this man was warned three or four times by nurses, but he just continued. Everyone in the Ward became annoyed with it.

The last I heard, is that he had to return, as something

had gone wrong with his procedure. No one was taking any notice of him this time. One or two people had stents fitted that went wrong and they had to return a couple times after collapsing. On the whole people were lovely in the hospital except for one brute without a brain.

"I know I shouldn't indulge myself in the TV lounge."

Well, why do it?

He was a nasty man. Frank and I decided to go and watch TV one evening. I think it was a science fiction film.

Frank only said "it's not my cup of tea" then suddenly this brute went overboard calling him all the names under the sun, using very foul language.

There are signs everywhere in the hospital, saying that anyone caught using such language, or causing problems would be severely dealt with by Internal Security, or the Police.

You meet all sorts, in those places.

I was still awaiting my date at Leeds. The day of extraction of my teeth was now here. A Nurse injected a local aesthetic to freeze my jaw.

"Can you feel this?"—"Can you feel that?"

"No," is my reply.

"Good we'll start."

I am not a lover of dentists, but I had to have it done before the operation could take place.

"You'll feel a crack."

It seemed to be all over in a flash.

My gums bled for a while, but they did not take too long to heal.

Eventually, the day arrived when I was due to be

transferred by ambulance to Leeds General Infirmary...

"Your due to leave for Leeds General Infirmary," advises a Nurse.

"When?" is my reply.

"Now."

I had to gather my things quickly as the Ambulance drivers were waiting to take me to Leeds General Infirmary.

I arrived in the early evening of 19th March 2018 at 19:34 p.m.

A Ward Sister admitted me into the High Dependency Ward in the Jubilee Wing. I had a room on my own next to the Nurse's station.

It was noisy as electronic warnings and alarms were going off all night.

I removed the large *ticking* clock on the wall and put it in a drawer.

Why do they have loud ticking clocks in Hospital rooms? They are so annoying and upsetting, especially at night, when you are trying to sleep. I also removed two other clocks from my earlier hospital.

I left the window open all night. I could hear babies crying and screaming. Was it the cry of a child or something more sinister? It sounded like someone was screaming, and it happened all over again on my second night... it turned out that my room was near the Maternity Wing and that it was expectant mothers in the labours of childbirth.

All the Doctors and Nurses were lovely. I was obviously frightened of the unknown and one Doctor reassured me that I was in safe hands saying they were "the best in their field" which helped.

The night before my operation my consultant came to see me and told me straight.

Life or death… living or dying… no beating about the bush.

He was straight to the point.

The Consultant told me plainly that I had two choices.

"You can stay as you are, but eventually time will run out, you will keel over and that would be that" or "If you have the operation, you'll feel like a new man."

He also informed me of a 9% chance of not making it.

I signed the paperwork, there and then, giving the consent to my operation. My life was now in God's hands.

The Consultant did not go too much into the procedure, except to say that I would be in theatre for eight hours, and that I would then go into Intensive Care for three weeks. He told me it would be an extraordinarily complex procedure.

The night before my operation I had to shower in a *pink liquid* from head to foot. The nurse informed that it would stop the "MRSA" bug. A Nurse told me that all my belongings would be removed by hand, logged by another Nurse, and put away for safe keeping in a holding area.

The next day arrived. It was the day of my operation.
Major Open-Heart Surgery.
The night before my operation I was having a panic

attack. Even though I am a firm believer in God and a Catholic, my nerves got the better of me.

"What if this is the last time I will be on earth?"

"What if I don't make it?"

A couple of Nurses calmed me down, and a doctor helped me overcome my nerves.

A kind of calm came over me, on the day of my operation. I made a good act of contrition before I went into theatre. Someone was talking about the "last rites" at the other hospital.

A Nurse gave me a sedative to "calm me down" for the operation. I got on to the trolly and I was on my way to theatre. I do not remember arriving there or anything about the operation.

I was out of it.

I had read that the medication they gave you was extraordinarily strong, it could give you nightmares and vivid dreams. I thought that I would have the dream of walking towards "the light" and someone telling me to "go back it's not your time yet."

Mine was different and quite the opposite. I was in an "induced coma," and I also contracted hospitalised pneumonia.

Someone told me, after their operation, they could see "ants and spiders" moving about.

Very creepy.

The dreams I had were vivid, they seemed real.

When you normally dream you can only remember fragments, but I remember exactly what happened in my coma.

So real, so life like, it is hard to know why.

They were real... with real people. You could touch them.

No tunnel... no white light... no one to greet me...

What happened to me in "my coma" happened for a reason.

BETWEEN WORLDS

This is what happened... and the truth...

A coffin splits in two then slams together to make one.
A nurse is sitting at my bedside.
I awake.
"I'm sorry you didn't make it... your dead."
"But I feel so alive."
"I'm your guide... your only halfway between."
HEAVEN and EARTH.
How can I be?
The nurse disappeared.

My consultant had told me that I would be in Intensive Care for 2–3 weeks and it would be on a one to one, basis. One nurse to each patient.

I was unaware I was in a coma. I could see them looking down at me, perfect white teeth, white or blue uniforms... they came and went.

I then had a terrible thought... THEY ARE ALL TRYING TO KILL ME!!!!

As weird as it was, it felt as if I was having sandy soil put into my mouth, down and down into the ground until I managed to get out again. The same dream would repeat itself over and over, again.

Everything was real. It was a horrible dream; then it seemed to pass.

I could see my surroundings, it was so vivid, so real, but was it true?

I felt alive, unaware I may be in another time... another place.

I thought… "there's been no funeral, it can't be real."

I somehow found my way to the Church of my birth in Batley and sure enough there had been no funeral. Nothing had taken place.

"So… I'm not dead?"

I could see my sister in my room—I was not there.

A coffin was in a side room. My Sister was sat beside it. I could not see any name plate on the coffin.

She suddenly ran out of the room.

I thought… "the coffin is for me."

I then seemed to travel to my sister's home. I could see the driveway; the door opened. All the lights were on, but no one was inside. It was all real and it felt real.

I thought… "I must be dead" but I had questions that needed answering.

Why didn't I go all the way?

Why am I only halfway?

Where is my Mum and Dad?

Am I only good enough to get halfway?

Was I being prepared?

I have been good all my life and done what is right… why was I only halfway?

Why were they trying to kill me?

No one was trying to kill me it was the medication.

In my coma what happened next was also very real. Someone called Jack, who was in hospital asked me if I would like to be one of the writers for a new updated version of THE PERSUADERS! Jack said that it had a £320,000,000 budget and Andy Latif at ITV had given the go ahead.

How could I say no?

I can find no evidence of Jack, Andy Latif or the £320,000,000 budget by ITV, but I must have believed it, because I started to write the first episodes on Leeds Teaching Hospitals notepaper, while in Intensive Care. It was all part of my coma. They didn't exist, yet they were real.

I had started to write an Episode and wording for the DVD launch. I had also recruited various characters from staff at the hospital.

"Jack" had said his son Jamie Pickford could play the Brett Sinclair role and I spotted a young male nurse who could take on the Danny Wilde role, not only that, but he also turned out to be his grandson.

It was an illusion.

I said... "We will have to change your name for the show, and it will reflect your grandfather and protect your real name."

TONY LEE CURTIS.

PERFECT.

We already had the Brett Sinclair car.

Where?

It was on my drive.

The car is worth £300,000. It was a gleaming gold Aston Martin. I would drive the car by road and store it in the South of France. I would also use it here too and assume the role of Brett Sinclair. My partner would be Lady Sinclair. We would move to a bigger house near Leeds/Bradford airport.

It was very strange, but it all felt real.

Was I delusional, was it all a dream?

Why was this happening?

I must have believed it, as I had started to write the show. I did not want to let Jack down. So much detail, so real, it felt real, I totally believed in it. I can only imagine what the Doctors and Nurses thought of me. I must have driven them mad; they went along with everything. I was living and breathing this show.

What happened to the Nurse at my bedside?

Was she an Angel?

So many Questions that need Answers?

...Yea though I walk in the valley of the shadow of death, I will fear no evil, for thou art with me, thy rod and staff comfort me... Psalm 23 – THE LORD IS MY SHEPHERD

COMA REVELATION

The dreams in my coma continued. Another strange dream was that somehow, part of the building in the hospital, went by road to the South of France... and ended up in Menton. It was in a car park on the seashore. Was I in a parallel World?

Someone was trying to extract money and the Doctors were trying to calm things down. I remember saying to a nurse,

"He's wearing Cuban heels and a crook."

It turned out he was one of the Doctor's too, but again it was all real. I thought at this stage, I was in the role of Brett Sinclair. I asked one of the nurses to get me a phone saying, I would ask Danny Wilde to sort things out. I seemed to be in the early Seventies.

Danny arrived eight hours late saying,

"OK where's the fire Charlie?"

My sister and partner had arrived by plane in Nice and were making their way down to Menton. Another illusion. I was still in Intensive Care at Leeds General Infirmary.

My coma lasted for a week. I was on a ventilator. It was Holy week at the time. I remember my partner saying...

"You know who I am don't you?"

My sister said I was "confused" and trying to get out of bed. The nurses in Intensive Care didn't allow that.

My Sister was right though I was confused, but it was all part of being in a coma and what happened after it.

All the Doctors and nurses in Intensive Care were wonderful and it was obvious that their method of going along with it worked.

I answered my sister saying... "I am not confused" and I distinctly remember that, but she was right I was confused, it was all down to my coma and the side effects of the strong medication.

The nurses gave me oxygen and I had to use breathing masks. The Ward Sister was constantly threatening me about keeping them on. It was general procedure. I was being a bit of a rebel.

Back in my coma, a "launch party" was being organised for the new show. I remember saying, that Tony's wife and daughter were visiting in the next bed. Everyone told me it is not them, but I insisted it was.

It was an elaborate party in my honour, and it felt very real. Two or three NHS workers were either part of, or married, to someone related to Tony's family.

It all seemed very real.

We were all going to see the launch party in Alassio Italy, that evening. It never happened because of thunderstorms. A Doctor arranged for us all to re-record The Persuaders theme in acapella. It was vastly different to the original!

We were all gathered in a type of recording area, all our families too. I remember a blonde nurse looking after me.

"That lady is your Mum," I said.

She said, "no she isn't."

I said, "she is."

Eventually she admitted she was. The Nurse probably said this to stop me from asking again. I recruited her to be *part of the team.*

Someone was giving out copies of The Persuaders original DVD's, mine said "Director" on it. I also had one of those "Director" type chairs with my name on it.

I couldn't find anything when I woke up.

They were all part of my coma.

I must have believed it all; there was so much detail, it was so very real. I felt alive. People were real and you could touch them. We were all alive.

How can it be a dream?

Why was this happening?

I used to watch The Persuaders, at the earlier hospital. My World being influenced by it at the time? I don't know the answer.

We also had a type of launch party at a French barn that served bacon and eggs. A nurse was trying to put on a Seventies dance track, but the machine kept it on hold.

I met another patient. I said that he would be perfect for another remake as his voice was like the character actor down to a tee. I do not remember who he was. It was all part of the vivid coma.

The Seventies dance track was in the original TV show, and it felt real.

The Seventies track is a type of dance. I remember Roger Moore's famous cringeworthy version in The Persuaders. I said that we would have it in the latest version, and it also would have an updated soundtrack.

Everything felt so real, it went on and on.

No one could get the Funky Chicken to play.

I was still in my bed clothes. It was all very embarrassing. Yet it was all real to me. It was all true. No bacon and eggs for me. The nurses wouldn't allow it. People were real and you could touch them, this was no dream.

It seemed, all of Tony's family were there too, and two or three of them worked for the NHS or were married to NHS workers, doctors, and nurses.

How can all of this be real?

My sister said that I was in an "induced coma" for a week in Intensive Care; she is a nurse with the NHS. It is incredible to think that "the brain" must have created all of this on its own, as the dreams were so vivid, and people were real. It was so very real to me.

I remember making a promise to the Ward Sister of £12,000,000 plus, 100,000 monitors and 100,000 keyboards, as well as new CPR beds.

The Ward Sister had manipulated me. Why didn't they just ask for it? The plan was for me to donate this to Leeds General Infirmary out of the receipt of funds from ITV.

In the cold light of day, I can find no trace of that at all, although it must have been real to me at the time. I realised, that the nurse who first appeared in my coma, was "not of this World."

I talked to various nurses and told them of my *coma experience* they were all flabbergasted. The Nurses advised that they didn't have the authority to inform me that I was dead and would never do this anyway. It became clear to me that the lady or nurse at my bedside was an *Angel*. She was not of this World. Angels do not appear in person, except in certain life changing circumstances. They can also take any form. Like most people I had never been in a coma or knew anything about them.

Now my life has changed; it will never be the same again.

THE GIFT OUT OF MY COMA

I did not realise it at the time, but something had happened to me after being in my coma, something had changed.

I started to write for the new 2018 version of The Persuaders! I thought that it was a dream too, until one day when I was leaving hospital and gathering my things together when, there it was, evidence of my writing on Leeds Teaching Hospital note paper.

I wrote it while in Intensive Care, it was real and true!

I remember thinking "I can't let Jack down and I must start to write it now."

This was early April 2018.

One of the nurses wearing a white tunic worked for the Leeds Teaching Hospital. I said she would be perfect for the new show, and it would appeal to a new audience in 2018. ITV wanted it as a rival to another show on another channel. We had a £320,000,000 budget, all provided by the advertising on ITV.

In truth it was not real, although to me, it was. My mind must have created it whilst I was in a coma. I never knew anything about that at all it just named me as Director. How could I re-write this show?

My nurse informed me that she was going to the Philippines in September. I advised that would be OK, as the filming on location would be "in the can" then.

We had no Film Director at that point. No writing done. I had to write it. I had never written for TV before, or at all really.

My nurse then shaved me. I must have had a week's

growth then. At one stage I felt as if I was part of filming for a TV Hospital show in Scarborough. I could hear boats in the harbour. In truth, it was the sound of the hospital generators below us.

I was not sure if this was real or not. I even thought that no operation had taken place, but I soon came to realise that it was real, when I looked at my chest.

So how can the rest of it not be real?

When you dream your lucky to remember fragments. They are not vivid enough to remember. When your "in a coma" you remember everything. You can touch people, everything is real.

It cannot be a dream. Is it a virtual reality?

There was someone in a bed next to me, who had an incurable disease. I said...

"If I find the answer I will return, and you will be cured."

What answer and how can I go back?

Strange but true.

I also thought it was New Year's Eve in Millennium Square and fireworks were going off.

I realised it was Easter in another strange dream. The *building* was back on the road from Italy to the UK.

"I don't have any passport."

"Don't worry we're going back by the shortest route. No passport is needed." A Doctor advises.

When the "building" eventually returned, it positioned itself next to Apperly Bridge railway station, near Leeds.

I was still in Intensive Care.

"I've got a feeling, call it what you will, that something is going to take place." I tried to get out of bed.

"Sorry, you can't get out of bed… Doctor's orders."

My partner was going back to work on Tuesday, it just happened to be the day of the warning, and she was at the train station.

The monitor recording my life sign readings was playing a different tune, in an odd sequence. It was The Persuaders theme?

"I've got a feeling that a bomb is going to go off." It was weird, but I trusted my instincts.

I do not know why I should feel like that. I know I tried to get out of bed, countless times, but the nurses would not let me. I told them of my vision and warning, but they kept me in bed. I was still rigged up to the lifesaving machine in Intensive Care.

I felt helpless. Time was running down to 6:00 a.m. I asked again to get out of bed. It was all part of the effects from my "induced coma."

Everything felt so real. I was living it. This was no dream.

I had no idea, at the time, this was "Another World" running alongside my own.

It got to 6:00 a.m. and of course, nothing happened.

How could it, I was still in Intensive Care at Leeds General Infirmary. It all felt real, but it was all in my mind, my brain had conjured it up.

My recollection of "The Angel" encounter was real. I had pre-warnings, years before my operation, and predictions in "my coma" turned into reality. I was in "Between Worlds." It had predicted the future and those predictions came true.

Months later, I found out that when you have your operation, you are put on *life support* by the Surgeons and a ventilator in the operating theatre. The Surgeons stop your heart, and in my case, my heart was stopped for eight hours!

My brain obviously thought I was dead, and I was, clinically dead. When you go into the Operating Theatre, there is a good chance that you may die as well as live, on that table.

My consultant informed me, prior to my leaving, that it had been "touch and go" during my operation. I was shocked to hear that.

I am so glad that God answered my prayers. My future somehow lies in my procedure.

I received "A Gift" out of being in a coma.

Just how I will use that gift, lies in the weeks and months that lie ahead.

REASONS

My "induced coma" lasted for over a week in Intensive Care. I had a mechanical Aortic valve fitted by Surgeons in an eight-hour long operation in March 2018.

They saved my life.

I know all my prayers have been answered, and I thank God for being alive, every day.

Whilst under the effects of the medication, my journey "Between Worlds" continued. My partner told me that I rang my sister, accusing her of killing the cat—I don't remember that at all, or when she came to see me on Holy Thursday and squeezed my hand.

It was the first time that I had missed all the Easter celebrations at Church, but I was out of it, in my own world, far away from normal reality.

My World then ran alongside my own.

In another side of the coma, I thought my sister had brought in a local paper saying that a Blackpool show was going to be revived at a disco called "Sixties Street." In the paper were old photos from sixty years ago.

I did wonder how it would work today. The Sixties era was such a unique time, and whilst we can revisit it in a musical, it would not work in 2018. I never found any evidence of this at all; another unexplained dream that felt real.

I decided to prove myself wrong and I wrote another six-part comedy drama out of "my Gift" called "Blackpool Rocks" based on my Sixties dream...

My story travels through the decades from the '50s into the Swinging '60s, then the '70s followed by the '80s.

It eventually arrives in 2020 at a party to end all parties.

This is my story… it highlights how things have changed through time. Remembering all the good times, reliving them through it all at the Swinging Sixties Show bar… then seeing what happens when a brand new 2020 version opens next to The Tower… and I'm running it…

You've got to be joking… right?

Prepare for the rollercoaster ride of your life… from the Tower Ballroom to the Pleasure Beach…

This really is the Blackpool story.

Hold on to your hats… Kiss me Quick… it's all here.

Back to The Persuaders! My brain, and mind were in overdrive. All the characters were real and various Doctors and nurses played their part, but I thought it to be real, as I had written part of the new 2018 version of The Persuaders!

Will ITV take it if I approach them? That lies in the future.

It was not long after coming round in Intensive Care that I started to write the updated version.

Now back at home, my journey has just begun on the road to recovery. How long it will take is anyone's guess. My scars and various bruises continue to heal quickly, although the mental scars will never fade. I am so grateful and thankful, as they all saved my life at Leeds General Infirmary. I owe them everything.

God was true to his word, and it was fulfilled when I survived. The dream I had in pictures, before I went into hospital, were all true. How can I ever repay that?

I am alive, you just cannot put a price on that. I

remember thinking, that money is no use to you, when you are going through a life changing operation. No one can help you. My faith was stronger than ever when I was going through it all, that is all that matters.

We are not alone. God gives us what we need, to get us through.

All the nurses were brilliant, nothing was too much for them and it was obvious they were specially trained in their field. They knew exactly how to treat each patient and care for their needs.

What happened to me in my coma has stayed with me.

I thought, I owe Leeds General Infirmary £12,000,000 plus all the other things I promised, just how am I ever going to get that done?

It was all part of "my coma."

I wrote earlier that I was on a journey and a leap into the unknown. Something wonderful, may come out of it in the weeks and months that lie ahead? I do not have to search for answers. My eyes have been opened on this matter.

These are the words I have written in a book capturing the events of "my coma."

Everything concerning my coma, has been recorded in detail.

My story continues...

I have now been in recovery for eight weeks. I am still in awe at the skill of the Surgeons in saving my life and God's promise in a dream has been fulfilled just as it was predicted on Friday 14th February 2018.

I am alive, in every sense of the word.

I am a new man.

I know I have a long way to go, but I am on the road to full recovery.

I now *carry the card* and must take Warfarin for the rest of my life. It is a small price to pay for being alive.

Life is so precious.

When you are in Hospital and you're told "you have two choices" money and everything else, is of no importance. It can no longer help you. No matter who you are, rich or poor, we all face the same choice "life or death," there are no other options. You know it when you are in hospital, and you're faced with exceptional circumstances. The facts are clearly set out before you.

"Choose Life" was the slogan T-shirt in the Eighties.

You know it was right.

I did not want to die.

I admire those who say, "well if it happens, it happens."

For all my religious beliefs and messages, I chose life. There is no other choice for me. I admire those older than me, but the little boy inside, is frightened of the unknown and it still burns bright.

My human side.

There is no escaping it.

God gives us what we need.

I am not looking to find all the answers just maybe to understand all I need to know.

Was I saved for a reason?

Maybe I'll find out in the months and years to come?

FIRST STEPS — A NEW ME

When you have had an operation of such magnitude, the first thing you must do, is get back on the road to recovery. I had to walk every day, even though it was for short distances for a while.

My consultant recommended only filling the kettle half full for a coffee or cup of tea, this was to allow the scar on my chest to heal without being too heavy.

I must make frequent visits to hospital locally, and back to Leeds General Infirmary for ongoing assessment and Cardiac care.

Astonishingly I found my first piece of writing on Leeds Teaching Hospital note paper when leaving the High Dependency ward. I decided to call my first script "Angel of Death" and I would maybe write another on completion.

I had never written books or for TV before. I never knew how. Now I think of the title first, then fit the story around it.

As I have said before, I am not a writer or reader of books, but I seem to have received this, as part of the wonderful things that happened to me in "my coma."

We will see where this dream takes me in the future.

When I was young, I used to see fortune tellers with my Mum in the 1960s. I have always been attracted to that side of things. There is something in it, I do not find it harmful at all.

After my Mum died in September 1987, I went to see a lady in Leeds, and she read my palm.

The Lady said the Lifeline on my left hand "was broken." She told me I would have a serious illness sometime in my life, but I would recover and go on to live a long life.

I only remembered that when I was in the High Dependency Ward. She was obviously talking about the here and now.

No heart attacks, no warning. If I had not been out of breath, I may never have found out. Things happen for a reason.

All the yearly blood tests I had with my GP, revealed nothing.

My blood pressure is back to normal today, in hospital it was often low, then high. No explanation. The Doctors were amazed; it seems to have gone back to its normal readings now. My consultant wants to bring it down even lower and that is now being worked on. It may involve taking stronger medication to do so.

God works in mysterious ways, His wonders to perform, and He worked a miracle into my life, saving me along with the Surgeons. I had to be *weaned off* the strong medication whilst in the induced coma.

Back in my book, my ongoing recovery stems from my time in High Dependency. I am on a *mashable* diet, which restricts you from having a normal type of meal, but I will go along with it for now. You must do as your told, doctors' orders.

The Ward Sister said that I also had a *vocal-chord palsy* this is in addition to having open-heart surgery.

I am due to have an X-ray on my throat.

My voice has always been *husky*. I knew they wanted

67

to check it out, so I decided to go along with their wishes, particularly if it helps me overall.

I am informed by the sister on the Ward in High Dependency, that I will have to do "more exercises" but no surgery will be required.

That was a huge relief.

I have been through the mill, call it what you will, all for my benefit of course. It was life changing. There was nothing I could have done to prevent it.

I decided to listen to all they had to say and take on board what it all meant, particularly if it enhanced my life.

It is true to say that I feel like a *new man* now. They were right. I am not out of breath, one bit.

My doctors instructed me to take it easy though, taking five minute's walking at a time, and then to build up on this.

Sadly, where I live there are a couple of hills.

I have been lucky with my life. I am still here.

I know that all could have been lost when I was in my coma, but God looked down and gave me life again. I have been blessed, knowing I can go on. I thank God every day for the wonderful thing He has done for me.

Were all the things I did in life correct and the decisions I made the right ones? I've made mistakes like everyone else.

God has rewarded me with life. I am so grateful for everything.

FALLING INTO PLACE

It seems that everyone, and everything, has played a part in my life. It all seems to have fallen into place.

My first appointment is to see The Consultant in Cardiology on 25th May 2018, at Leeds General Infirmary. It takes place in the Jubilee Wing, and it is my first check over. I seem to be doing well and my scars are healing nicely. Confidence has grown, since my first tentative steps, with the tripod. I was soon walking up and down the hospital corridors and I grew to walk unaided. Now I can walk normally but I must build up slowly five minutes at a time.

A Cardiac Nurse visited me on 24th April 2018 and said everything was as it should be. My blood pressure and pulse were both normal. Sleeping and taking it easy, is the order of the day.

You could say, I have been through the equivalent of a car smash, and I must learn to walk, before I can run. I have accepted that it will take time, and it may take the rest of the year to get back to how I was.

I am glad to be alive.

I do not know why it happened to me, but if it hadn't happened, I may not be here now. I know things happen for a reason, which are sometimes beyond our control. I know I could have died from it, but I was lucky. Other people might say, I was incredibly lucky indeed. Someone was watching over me, there's no doubt about that.

There are so many unanswered Questions. Each day is a bonus. You must accept life for what it is, and for the best. I realise I have now been given a *second chance*.

My premonition was true.

I am living proof.

I know I must take Warfarin for the rest of my life, but it is a small price to pay. It regulates the flow of blood and prevents clots. I now have a mechanical aortic valve and the levels of warfarin need to be checked often at my local Hospital to see that it is performing.

They are all experts in their field. The Nurses said that it is customary practice for it to fluctuate until they find the right dosage for me. Everyone is different. You must do as your told and I am no exception.

I have written my first TV script which is based on my vivid dreams whilst in an induced coma.

I decided to call it "Angel of Death" which is different to what happened at the time.

The "Angel" that appeared to me in "my coma" was quite the opposite. I remember she had a *white gleaming robe*. She was pretty, but my recollection of anything else is misty, as she virtually disappeared, after delivering her words concerning my life.

The story has been adapted for my new 2018 version of The Persuaders! I find it easier to write TV scripts than to write books.

I do not know at this stage whether it is a one off, or if it will develop into something more. I have five more titles ready to be scripted, I do not know why this is happening?

My life will never be the same again. Everything has changed.

My consultant says that I must not drive until August,

and to avoid picking up or lifting heavy objects. The reason being is that after having an open-heart operation, this refers to when the chest's opened, and when the Surgeons leading the operation is conducted. A period of three months is needed for things to heal.

I began to write my "Angel of Death" script in the TV room, while I was waiting for transport to arrive, on 12th April 2018 to take me home, from Leeds General Infirmary. It did not take long to finish it. I suppose it was because, everything felt so real to me.

I have another five titles in production, they all just need to be script written. They can be adapted for any drama. I never thought I would ever do anything like this.

The "Gift" out of my coma has created all of this. I want to make it a reality.

Where will it all lead?

My TV scripts are *all* original and have been written for the future.

Who knows where that will take me?

After writing The Persuaders, it became clear to me, that I needed to write my own *original* dramas.

I decided to write "It's a kind of Love" based on my own story. It is about a man who decides to change his social life, when he joins a national Singles organisation in Leeds. It changed my life. I had heard *a song* on the radio in early 2017. Whenever I heard it, that song reminded me of all those happy times I had there. Today's internet and speed dating are no match.

"It's a kind of Love"—This is how it all began...
It's back to 1987 for this twelve-part comedy drama

set in Leeds. It is based on a true and original story up to the end of 1991... what happens after that continues in the next series.

Gez tells his story and meets Mike... together they highlight events at Zodiac Mirage Singles Club... with amazing success.

I could go into raptures about my time there. I met so many wonderful people. They became a huge part of my life. I have enormous respect and love for them all.

I decided my next series would have the title of "Beyond Time." I wrote this in July 2018 in twelve parts.

"Beyond Time."—Picture the scene...

It's July 2018, I'm sat in a garden chair on my balcony. It's a hot summer's day; I fall asleep in my chair. When I awake it's July 1968...? I am fourteen, and 2018 is fifty years in the future. What's happened?

Have I found my perfect Heaven... and just how do I return to present day 2018?

...and do I really want to go back?

In this drama I relive being back at college, starting work, and all the things I did in my life. There is just one rule, *don't* interfere with time to do so, will change the future.

It is a rollercoaster ride, but fun reliving all that I have done from my past. I am just so amazed that my brain has recorded and kept all those memories.

As for getting back to 2018... anything is possible in fiction.

With regards my next two dramas I decided to write

about my "Gift" and coma experience. "Forever and Ever" is another twelve-part series.

"Forever and Ever"—Picture the scene...

The setting is Batley, West Yorkshire. The drama is set around a local parish and the parochial Hall. Gez has received a great gift. After consulting with the Parish Priest an eventual meeting is set up to meet The Bishop. As the fame spreads, an audience at The Vatican awaits.

"In a Coma" is also a unique twelve-part drama. It is all about faith and beliefs. What would you do with the choices I've received or dealt with in life?

This drama weaves in and out of normal life, yet there is nothing normal in this story. Truth and reality are what it is all about.

...and a major question...

WHAT WOULD YOU DO IF GOD SPOKE TO YOU THROUGH HIS MESSENGER?

Well, what would you do?

I dramatized, my own experience, of being in a coma. It was an early attempt at writing something original. Everything I had gone through was in this drama.

My next two dramas were about angels.

I decided to write "Angel's Eyes" and follow it with "Christmas Angels."

I wrote my series of "Angel's Eyes" in twelve-parts and set it in Leeds and York.

Everything has a wonderful *Yorkshire* feeling to it.

Michael the Arc Angel sends four real Angels, to undertake all types of problems, in a modern-day setting.

Will they rise to the challenge? Are they clever enough to do so, while undercover as humans?

I really enjoyed writing this series, as I could incorporate, and weave different stories, into each episode.

"Angel's Eyes"—This is what I wrote...

Opening Episode—"It's written in the stars"

The eyes are the windows of the soul. God's mission. Human form on earth. God is God. Tell them—I have sent you. Angel introductions. Receiving the Holy Spirit. No suspicions. Healing broken lives. Bringing them back to God's Kingdom. Sins retained. Park Square, Leeds. The Convent, York. Ghostly apparitions. Total protection. Lost souls.

"Christmas Angels" is also a four-part series set in York. This series reunites Rebecca, Mary, John Paul, and Nicola. They assume the role of proprietors at a shop in York. Various human, and angelic encounters take place... all with a magical Christmas feeling.

I lost a lot of weight whilst being in hospital, at one stage, down to 11st 10lb! I have not been like that since being in my twenties.

My feet ballooned in Hospital. The Doctors said that this was down to having heart failure. My Consultant said that my heart was "not doing what it should do" and that, is the failure.

I do not remember my life "flashing before me" as the saying goes. Nothing like that, happened to me. God helped me, more than I can say. I was helped that's for sure. The premonition I had in a dream prior to going into hospital showed the truth, and it came true. I knew I was going to live again, because God had said so, even though I thought I was going to die.

It was not my time.

I thank God every day, and the brilliance of the Surgeons.

How can I ever repay it?

By living a good life. I am hoping I can repay that out of the "Gift" in my coma.

I wonder what God has in store for me.

Somehow, I feel changed, a different person.

Something wonderful, happened to me in my coma.

My child-like journey continues, on another path, another level. In the weeks, months, and years ahead I may find the answer?

You only need faith to believe. You only need to believe to have faith. I genuinely believe.

LIVING PROOF

It is now 3rd May 2018, and here I am living proof, premonition fulfilled, alive and kicking.

God's promise to me is now a reality.

The Surgeon's put me back together. The Doctors and nurses in Intensive Care were all wonderful. I love them all. I owe my life to their skills at Leeds General Infirmary.

Was I really on the cusp of leaving this World?

I will never know the answer to that question, or how lucky I was on the verge of life or death. I am so grateful to all those people involved in my recovery. You feel part of *their* family.

If you are doubting your future or without belief, I hope my story will inspire you all, and change your lives.

This book is about truth and reality.

I have five projects in the pipeline now. Not bad for someone who does not write books or read them.

A Gift?

Perhaps.

I have continued to write my TV scripts and now have five new stories. I am still a novice at this. I decide on the titles and the story lines, which is the easy part.

The next thing is to try and write it. I never get *writer's block.*

My new project is based on my time when I was a member of a Singles Organization in Leeds from 1987 to 1993. There is no time limit, it will be full of timeless characters, based on a true story.

My story.

All the characters are real, and events and story lines

are real. Eighties music will feature throughout. The inspiration to write it goes back to 2017 when I heard a certain song on the radio. I am not a lover of "music while you work" but this piece of music was upbeat, it reminded me of my time in Leeds. The music had worked its magic. Whenever I heard it on the radio my mind was back to my time there. I had to do it. I had to write a book about my time there.

I decided to write a TV script in twelve parts. I blended it with real stories and some invented story lines but mostly it would be my story of that era, the late 1980s.

TV scripts are much easier to write than books. They are usually up to an hour long. The characters, dialogue and locations are key to the story lines. I fully intend to see this through.

This series could go on and on. I have given it a provisional title of "It's a kind of Love" and I suppose it was. The love of my life, at the time.

I sent a "sample script" to a well-known TV writer and they "liked it." High praise indeed for someone who had never written before. It could work and come to fruition, in the future. Watch this space.

I do not plan anything. Everything is a blank canvas, the very same as drafting a book.

It is not the case of *being in the mood* as to when something comes to me, then I take pen to paper.

It is as simple as that.

It is usually not long before that happens, and a wealth of words or ideas come to mind and then I begin to write it.

There is no magic formula.

All of this has come out of "my coma."

My stories are genuine and real, although my TV scripts may have a flavour "of the unknown" and will be fiction based on a sort of reality. Fiction based on fact. That is how I describe them. It is all "A Gift" and I will be over the moon, if my work is recognised even for TV, as I am not a writer at all.

Sometimes I may be watching something on TV when suddenly the next title *jumps* out from the screen. That is just how it happens, or I may simply think of something that might work and then latch on to that idea and take it from there.

It is a kind of inspiration.

It works for me.

As I have said before, there is no magic formula, it simply comes to fruition and that is all it takes.

CONTINUING CARE

Although I am in recovery, I still must return to Leeds General Infirmary for an X-ray on my vocal cords. I think I have always had a husky voice, but that is me. It is not a deep voice, it's always been like that. I am continuing with my exercises and living on a fork *mashable* diet and still following the guide rules until the nurses instruct me otherwise at my local hospital.

It is a waiting game, although the Doctors assure me that no surgery will take place.

It is also unlikely, that I will return to work. I am at retirement age and it seems the right thing to do, after going through such a trauma. It is time to move on. I have had a massive warning.

I am amazed by people's reaction and how they talk about dying "as a matter of fact." In reality, and the cold light of day, you are in a death defining stage of your life. What happened to me is extraordinary. There is no explanation. No human explanation.

My sister has gone into hospital, 8th May 2018, with a suspected appendix murmur, although they are doing more tests to find out why she is experiencing pain in this area.

I have put my faith in God, knowing that everything that happened to me, was for a reason. I may have had this all my life. I am no longer out of breath when walking, even though this is early days, I know you cannot run, before you can walk. I would say that deciding to retire, was an easy decision for me, influenced by having major open-heart surgery at Leeds General Infirmary. I am always amazed by remarks as "you were really poorly" and two or three people have even said "we didn't think you would make it"—I can see their point of view.

As for the future, I fully intend to progress my writing for TV.

My sister is now home, having left the hospital and tests are still on-going.

There is so much in life to look forward to. I do not know what God has waiting for me in the future. God works in mysterious ways His wonders to perform.

I am slowly progressing on the path to full health.

I live on a private estate, the land of which was once the home to a hospital. It was built in the 1920s and occupied a large piece of land. Now, there are two housing developments in its place. All the roads on the estate were named after the wards in the old hospital—by the Builder. My home is on the upper part and is found near to the nurses old changing quarters.

All sorts of *unexplained* things have happened since living here. Lights and electrical equipment, flashing on and off, between 8:00 p.m. and 8:35 p.m. which has become a strange sort of ritual; I notice it mostly during dark nights, when the lights are full on.

"The Grey Lady" still walks the wards of the old hospital, even though it was demolished over twenty years ago, and she still comes over the road to the old nurses quarters to get ready.

My house is slap bang in the middle of that. There is no escape.

Fortunately, I am not worried by such unexplained happenings. Strange but true, but after living here for over twenty years, I'm used to *unexplained* phenomenon.

"It's the living, not the dead that you have to worry about." My Mum used to tell me.

I am now of a *certain age* where I need to take care of myself, and if I follow the rules, I will get through it all. I do not know if everything I have been through, is down to being hereditary. I have never smoked in my life, have only a rare glass of wine, eat healthy food, plenty of fruit and vegetables which are all considered to live a good and healthy life.

We are all given a purpose in life. We are each given a gift.

Today we live in a World, of advanced technology. I do not think I would have been alive today, had it happened say twenty or thirty years ago. Advancement has allowed all of that to happen. We take things for granted today, but in truth it is a remarkable scientific achievement that works, and it will only get better in the years to come.

There have been giant strides in medicine and technology, although two or three of the older procedures remain, in medication, digoxin, and Warfarin for instance; they were in existence, and first introduced, over fifty years ago. Which goes to show... "if it's not broken don't try to fix it."

My new valve originates from Texas, in the US of A, so

if I start speaking in a different accent you'll know why.

Whilst in the High Dependency ward at Leeds General Infirmary I remembered a prediction made back in 1987. I had my palm read by a lady in Leeds, she told me that the lifeline on my left hand was broken.

"You are going to have an illness sometime in your life, but you will recover from it and go on to live a long life."

Yes, it is true my lifeline is broken.

Most people I have talked to have a full unbroken lifeline; trust me to be different though. All these things happen for a reason, and then we look for answers. I know I did, but the answer lies with me and no one else. I feel that I have moved on and God has given me a second chance.

I have cheated death twice now. The first time was in 2015 when I had a type of migraine. It was the type with the *flashing lights* that close in on you. It was early Saturday morning. I remember putting the kettle on to make a cup of coffee. Suddenly, something seemed to click or change. I did not know it at the time, but I had suffered a type of stroke. There was only the cat and me in the house.

I could not walk; it was as if I were on the moon trying to take giant strides and my arm was unable to pour the water from the kettle into the cup. The water was running all over the place. I checked my face in the mirror and I saw that the right-hand side was drooping and sullen.

All of this lasted just a few minutes. I managed to climb the stairs and I used my mobile to phone 999 for an

Ambulance. Three or four minutes later the Ambulance Responder and Paramedics were at my home, followed closely by another emergency ambulance. They thoroughly checked me out. The Paramedics took me by ambulance to my local hospital where I spent over five hours with doctors who investigated in A&E. A Doctor eventually told me, that I had a TIA (transient ischemic attack) brought on by my migraine. The Doctor told me to walk up and down the ward and then told me I was ok to leave. I returned to work on Monday morning.

Another "sign" awaited me when I got into the ambulance.

There was a medical bag in front of me, part of the lettering was hidden from view, I could read ESUS. I took it to mean that JESUS was watching over me.

The messages continue to take place. The last one was on 16th February 2018 when I received a premonition in a dream—showing me alive and well in the future; they take place approximately twice a year. I never get chance to question who delivers those messages. They all happen at the point of waking from sleep and this is so that I will remember them in detail.

All I can say is that I truly, believe in them. I am not sure why I have been chosen to receive messages like this.

It is all part of a "gift" that has been given to me.

It is known that angels relay God's message to us and through their messages we are connected to Heaven.

My hope is that these messages continue for the rest of my life.

Am I living the dream?

I know I will somehow make it a reality. My TV script writing continues to prosper, and I know, I will write all thirty-two episodes for the updated version of The Persuaders! I cannot explain it, but I must have to do this for a reason. It is to fulfil the promise that was given to me, all I know is that I will do it. Storylines are now in place.

Something wonderful, happened today 15th May 2018! A wooden angel figure carrying a candle next to my Mum and Dad's wedding photo became suddenly *surrounded* by light after I opened the curtains in our living room.

All these things mean and say something.

You only need to read "the signs."

Finding an answer is not easy, you just must keep believing.

Faith is the answer.

As followers of Jesus, we are journeying towards the sunrise, not the sunset. Our lives are short, three score and ten, it says in the Bible. What we have done in our lives will reflect on what happens to us; I believe most people have lived good and fulfilling lives.

I know we will all get our reward, as and when that time comes. All you need to do is believe, trust, and have faith.

INTO THE FUTURE

Where the future will take me is unknown, but I do know that things have changed for the better. I know that if all those things had not happened, I would never have known, and who knows, I could have and would have died.

What a thought, a very unpleasant thought. I would have been mortified yet I would not have been here, would I?

I am alive and that is all that matters.

It's what I do now, that I have got to figure out.

I am on a slow road to recovery, there is no time scale when you have had major open-heart surgery. Your body must accept that a foreign type of entity has been introduced into it and in my case, a mechanical Aortic Valve replacement.

Three or four weeks in and I must go to hospital on a weekly basis to have blood samples taken for my warfarin results. Target 2.5 – 3.0ml.

My readings have varied but no doubt they will steady as I progress. You must trust the Hospital's judgement on this one. I am walking well now, but I have not strayed too far from home.

I am thinking of drafting another book. I feel as though I have been "touched by the finger of God" and my life will never be the same again.

My *telepathic* dreams are just that, the unexplained, yet very real in what they say.

It is true to say that I feel that I have been influenced and helped by someone, on many occasions—in some way or another.

Four or five people I have spoken to, after coming home from Leeds General Infirmary, are amazed by "my story" and the very fact that I cheated death twice!

It is all true and very real. I hope it will inspire them to know that life is very precious. It's what we do in our lives that count, while we are here. No doubt it will stand us all in good stead.

I thank God, every day, for my life and for my "second chance."

Destiny is not a word I use at all, but I feel as though I am being guided by someone with a new beginning.

I am not interested in fame and fortune, only in truth and what is real. Fame and fortune are for those seeking something quite different.

What I have is a "Gift" that is for sure. It is not something you can buy. It must be earned; just how I managed to do that is a mystery at this time, but I am sure it will unfold as I progress.

I have looked for answers, but so far, I have not found any. The only answer I can find, comes back to me. Who I am, what I have done, my faith, my good life, it all must be part of the answer? Please, don't get me wrong, I have made mistakes in the past, like all humans do, but I have learned from them and put them right. We are all learning every day, how to live our lives. There are no "golden rules."

If people were amazed by "my story" in hospital it may have been down to destiny. Where I am going and what I must do, will no doubt come to me in the weeks, months and years that lie ahead.

I grew up in the Sixties, a world away from today.

It was a different time, a different era. They now call them "the post war years" which of course they were not. I have always tried to keep myself of good character and that still is relevant to this day. Believer, or not.

Our lives are moulded from birth, the roads that we are to take, for instance, our heritage and inherited bits and pieces. As for me, I never knew about what was to come, except for a prediction in 1987 by a palm reader.

I knew nothing of the irregular heartbeat or heart murmur in my life, it was an absolute shock. It came completely unexpectedly.

I have recently been to see my doctor, 21st May 2018, and found out that when I was in Intensive Care, I was *very* poorly. It's strange but until someone tells you, you do not think of yourself being this way at the time. All you focus on is getting better.

My heart was rejecting the new valve. The Aortic valve is one of the largest to replace. Can my story get any more complicated?

It has only been eight weeks since my operation, and I am due to meet with my Consultant in Leeds on 23rd May 2018. I am also due to have a check on my kidneys, post cardiac surgery; I may have to take further medication for this if prescribed by my doctor. All of this reminds you just how fragile we all are. God knows the answer. It seems I was "on the brink" but He answered my prayers. I received life to continue.

Jesus said to Mary Magdalene "your faith has saved you, go and sin no more."

I feel that my faith has saved me. There is no need to

look for explanations, there is nothing greater than love and faith. Mine continues to grow stronger, and I know I must place all my trust in God for the future, however long that is.

I think part of the mechanical valve rejection, initially by my heart, is common. If you think about it, you are having a foreign entity take the place of a real valve and that is why it takes time for the heart to accept it.

I seemed to be having heart failure all over the place!

The term "heart failure" means having breathlessness, swollen ankles; it does not mean that the heart has stopped working but that it has "failed" your body.

Frightening as it may sound, I was unprepared for it, I think anyone would be in that situation.

Somehow, I know, I will never be the same again.

For the next three nights, 22nd to 24th May 2018, there is a medical programme on national television in A&E (Accident and Emergency). My thoughts on it are that it might be too *raw* for me, too upsetting, but then, when I saw where it was coming from, I just had to watch it.

LIVE from LEEDS GENERAL INFIRMARY

My heart and soul are now part of what they do. It is a strange thing to say, but you feel a connection, as if your part of a huge family, and family ties matter. I know I belong to that close family.

I felt it compulsory to watch their skills and dedication. I am not fazed by it at all. I would say that belonging to a close-knit community is all that matters. I must make an emotional return on 25th May 2018, to see The Cardiac Team—one of countless visits.

Watching the medical programme *live* was compelling.

In A&E anything could happen, and it did. The "red phone" rang every five minutes, this meant the Air Ambulance was on its way or an ambulance on the road was due with critically injured people. It was "near to the bone" especially as I have only just been in that position, being eight weeks since my operation. They were all, as calm as ever. Doctors said that the Leeds General Infirmary was the number one in Yorkshire. I, fully agree with that, all the staff, doctors and nurses are totally dedicated to each patient, me included. Intensive Care and High Dependency had wonderful, resolute staff.

I will always, sing their praises.

I admit, I had to turn off the TV, as the programme was referring to blood and heart problems.

Mine was miraculous, to say the least.

WISE WORDS AND AMBITION

Ambition can be dangerous. It is true to say my ambitions are very real. I am hoping that I can eventually get my books and TV scripts over the line, with publishers/agents and TV companies; If this happens, it will be the "icing on the cake."

All my writing has come out of nowhere. Luck has something to do with it. Everything is out of my "Gift." Telepathy, premonitions, messages in dreams, what I have is special. It may take someone special to realise and see that. Like me, God will have touched their lives. They will need to believe and have faith in my projects. I hope this will happen—it is just a matter of time.

Today, Friday 25th May 2018, I have had a six-weekly assessment about my Cardiac surgery, with my Consultant in the Jubilee Wing of Leeds General Infirmary. The Consultant said that everything was ok with my surgery, and I must return in three months for a "gel type" scan on my chest to see if everything is progressing, then I will be fully discharged.

As promised, I returned to my Cardiac ward on "C" floor Intensive Care (Ward 6) and like me there were four or five poor souls going through what I had gone through, eight weeks ago.

Everything was real after returning to Ward 6. I did not dream those people up in my coma, they all actually exist. There they were, all real, and in the flesh. A nurse remembered, I offered him a staggering £1,000,000 to be in the updated version of The Persuaders! I was just over the moon that those people were real. I thought, I had not invented it, it really happened, but you know how your brain can play tricks on you.

Everyone remembered me, for all my talk of The Persuaders and the remake. Remarkable, it was so amazing. My brain recorded everything, whilst in a coma, and it was all real and the truth in lots of ways.

I have obviously said that I will keep them informed of any potential contract with ITV or for any other TV company for that matter.

I returned to the High Dependency ward (16) and thanked everyone there. Wonderful people, they all remembered me too. I even bumped into one of my fellow patients, whilst on the ward and he looked very well.

A modern-day miracle happened to me.

Can there be any more twists and turns to my story? I am sure there will be one way or another. It is not over by a long way. This may be just the beginning.

Why all of this has happened to me is a mystery, and always will be. It is never going to be over. There will be no end, all I can see is a continuation; things happen for a reason, I am certain of that. Whether I was chosen, I am not sure, and I will never know the answer to that at all. Only God knows the answer.

I am so grateful for all that has happened to me, the very fact that my life has been saved by everyone, makes it even more incredibly special.

I am turning my newfound skills into reality. My wish is that someone, will pick up my writing for development. I have written five TV scripts for the new version of The Persuaders to date, 31st May 2018. I have tried to weave quality into them; I am pleased with the outcome, so far. I have another twenty-seven to write and I will ensure they are all the same quality. I have stayed true to the original series, and kept to similar story lines, also injecting humour into the dialogue. It has been a revelation to me, as I have never written anything before, but now it's suddenly taking shape.

I have just remembered, back in the Eighties I had taken my car into a local garage for a full service and MOT.

My brother-in-law asked, "Did you know that the brakes had gone on your car?"

"No." I replied.

The Garage owner said I was "the luckiest man alive to have got there in one piece!" This was another unexplained mystery, which happened in my life.

I also remember going out in my brother-in-law's car back in the seventies when a similar thing happened, the brakes went while coming down Geldard Road near the Coach and Six traffic lights. Luckily, he used the hand brake and the kerb to stop the vehicle.

Another lifesaving mystery.

Things like this happen for a reason.

What happened to me, is a modern-day miracle.

A guiding light is now present. My Guardian Angel is very real and has found a way of communicating with me through dreams and saying the most extraordinary things too.

It does not matter, if no one believes me. I believe and that is all that matters.

Sadly, we live in a World that needs proof and evidence, which is the way it is. Everything that has happened to me is the truth. I just could not lie about such things.

Why would I?

All you must do is, open your hearts to accept the truth.

I continue to write, that is my legacy; what I write in my scripts and dramas is based on the truth. It may be easier to speak through my writings to get my point over.

The Gift—the brain—the coma as I refer to it, continues to grow and quite simply delivers the most demanding of drama.

My "Gift" seemingly wants to write about "The Saviour's Coming—The Second Coming" next; how I am going to write about that is a mystery to me. I just turn up and "The Gift" does the rest.

Unbelievable but true.

STORIES FROM THE HEART

I have now written five newly created dramas set in Leeds and the surrounding areas, together with thirty-three brand new episodes of The Persuaders! set on the French and Italian Riviera's and the UK.

All of this has come out of my coma, and it has a grip on all my emotions. The five created dramas are set in West Yorkshire and all original. I know it may be a strange thing to say, but the gift is getting stronger in content.

There is no stopping this very real roller coaster.

Just like my books, I write from the heart, nothing is false.

My dramas are based on my true story.

I feel reborn, a new man. I must use my gift wisely.

When I write my TV scripts, I follow my instincts. I decide on the title first, then write story lines in a book to follow. I then decide how many episodes to write, choose their titles, and then and only then, write my episode around each individual title.

I have gone from a blank canvas to a challenging and engaging story, and they usually are.

I have even written for old TV series. I am currently writing twelve brand new episodes of The Champions last seen on TV in 1968. It will be a new series reborn—for a new generation.

All of this has come out of my coma.

There is no end in sight at all to any of this. Everything continues and it has a firm belief that progress will be made. I am extremely enthusiastic about it.

The Gift has now become the core to everything, and I

must see it through no matter how long it takes or what shape it will form. It is all for the greater good.

My life is on a path that is set for the future.

The very fact that I survived open heart surgery in March 2018 is testament to it all.

I wanted to live. It was as simple as that.

I lost count of the times, I visited the chapel in hospital, asking God to save me.

I said, "I'll do anything in return."

My Gift is that challenge and to raise funds for Leeds General Infirmary's pioneering Heart units.

Sadly, I could not help my sister. She died on 31st August 2018 of terminal cancer.

We were always close. There is nothing you can do when that happens; you are unable to do anything.

I am the last man standing.

My faith and beliefs have always been important to me and since my own brush with death, they have become even more so. I have recently returned to Genetics/Cardiac at Leeds General Infirmary. They said my situation was all hereditary. It all happened in the first five weeks of conception—long before birth. I never knew about it.

Most people have three chambers in the Aortic valve, mine had only two. I am not alone, 2% of the population have the same defect. Many people do not know it yet, and may just continue or like me, they will have to have modern day surgery to rectify it.

My life has never been simple. The Consultant in Genetics said that it was not down to what I had eaten.

Luckily, I had never, ever smoked and only had the odd, rare glass of wine, eaten healthily, had plenty of vegetables and fruit, it all worked in my favour. It saved my life.

My lady Consultant told me, "I had done the right things." This was a genetic defect, a rogue gene that had done all of this, nothing else.

Trust me to be different; I could not have prevented it.

My vocal cord palsy was also down to the surgery, along with the wires I had in my throat.

I am glad to say that in early January 2019 I am back to normal, and my vocal cord is too. Yet normality is vastly different for me now.

I must take care of my heart and still attend clinic appointments at Leeds General Infirmary and my local hospital. I must take Warfarin for the rest of my life.

Everything is working, although I have not researched any of the medication I am taking, which is nine tablets a day. This is a small price to pay, for staying alive.

The magnitude of all that has taken place is really upsetting, yet it all had to be done by the Surgeons, to save my life.

As my story unfolds, I find that I can write at speed, this is more than likely to be part of "The Gift" out of my coma. I feel as if I am one of God's ambassadors on earth, I will tell my story to anyone who will listen.

No doubt my story will take even more twists and turns in the future. No one knows what is around the corner. I only know I certainly didn't.

As a New Year unfolds will I find out more answers?

I expect that more challenges lie ahead.
I am hoping my TV script writing will take off.
Who knows where that will take me?

GUIDING LIGHT

It is true, we all have Guardian angels in our life.

A gifted clairvoyant recently said that I have a guide and a spiritual guide.

Two angels are watching over me.

My Mum is especially watching over me, and she was true to her word in mid-October 1987 when she said,

"You think I've gone but I'm still here and I'm still watching over you."

That was thirty-two years ago.

I have felt her presence through all that time.

Recently, on Saturday 5th January 2019 when taking down our Christmas trimmings and tree, an angel wing ornament fell from the tree as I walked past. Is it another sign?

Lights on the outside balcony that had not worked for ages suddenly spun into life and were flashing at dusk, yet another sign.

I am a firm believer, honest.

On Sunday 6th January (The Epiphany) the lights were again flashing on at dusk and the other garden lights were lit even though we had no sunshine being in the dead of winter; they are solar operated. All these things continue to fascinate me.

For the first time in my life, I am on my own, yet I feel spiritually guided, spiritually connected.

It is unreal to think I am the last man standing in my family. I guess it's all inevitable really that one day the youngest, will be alone in the future. I am not really on my own, I have my wonderful partner, my soul mate, she really is my family.

I also class those in the Cardiac and Intensive Care, doctors, nurses, and the Consultants to be among my newly acquired family, also those in the High Dependency ward at Leeds General Infirmary.

I am not alone. You are only alone if you believe you are.

I was afraid of dying and all that it entails, even though I have been blessed by God with what happened to me in my coma. I am less frightened now.

No one wants to die. I know I certainly did not.

My sister wanted to die. She had terminal cancer.

I never thought she would die of that. It is extremely hard to get my head round it. She would have lived longer had she not smoked; I have never smoked, and this somehow went in my favour.

Guardian angels are watching over me. I know they are. I do not need visual evidence, which would be the icing on the cake. They only appear in extreme circumstances.

I did have an angel when I was in my coma. She was pretty and dressed in gleaming white. I only recently understood that she was a *real* angel.

After being in my coma and having my *revelation*, I spent the rest of the year wondering why this had happened.

I found out the answer in November.

A TV programme was being broadcast over three

nights called "Operation Live." In the first programme, it was the replacement of the Aortic valve, just like my operation. What I did not know, until then, was that they must—stop the heart, (eight hours in my case) then restart it when surgery has been completed.

You are on a machine or life support when the procedure is being conducted. Your brain obviously, continues to function.

The girl in my coma was human, a real angel. Everyone in my coma was real, you could touch them. I had found the answer to all my questions and so far, everything that took place has come true.

I know it is a big ask to get my TV scripts to the screen, but it is all a "Gift" out of my coma. The very fact that I have written all those dramas is a gift.

It continues, in my kind of Heaven, it is in control, not me.

Everything is real and nothing is false in my story.

With regards to my valve, I guess I could have gone at any time.

My guiding light has always watched over me. There have been countless times when I have felt—I was helped. A sixth sense tells me this is true; they are still watching over me now.

It really is no secret, that angels *really do* exist.

The unexplained, flashing lights on the balcony, messages in dreams, all continue to come my way. I did wonder if they were a warning of some kind, or an insight into what Heaven is really like. Were they sent to comfort me and prepare me for what was to come? All I know is that everything has changed for the better.

Now a year on, I am looking and feeling good. I am never out of breath, and I can walk long distances. Doctors constantly monitor me at Leeds General Infirmary. I am also checked by the Cardiac Consultants, and at my local hospital.

I asked The Registrar at Leeds General Infirmary,

"Why do I have to go there and not my local hospital."

He replied, "we are the surgeons, they are the doctors."

There was no answer to that.

OMENS

Messages in dreams continue.

Another thing happened when I was out…

This is what occurred … 25th July 2018. I bought a checked shirt from a local Charity shop it was brand new and had never been worn. It had an Italian label. When I arrived home, I looked at the label inside… it had my name on it.

G Cullen.

Well, I had not put it there.

There is a million to one chance of that ever happening. Is someone trying to tell me something?

That has never happened to me before.

Is it an omen?

Wednesday 8th August 2018. I had a vivid dream in the afternoon whilst taking a nap…

I was back with my Mum and Dad in our old house, only it was not the same. I asked my dad about the stained-glass window in the kitchen being so large and vivid.

Someone said,

"Your Mum is asking for you upstairs." It was my aunt. I never got there.

It was so vivid and real—as it was in my coma.

My Mum died in 1987 and my dad died in 1980.

Sometimes it feels like time is standing still, while other times it's as if time flies.

I am extremely fortunate; I can still recall memories from over fifty years ago. The coma did nothing to erase that at all. If anything, I would say that it has strengthened my memories of everything.

Angels continue to speak in my dreams, I cannot stop them. I never get chance to speak to them or ask who they are. It is very much one way traffic; they are totally in control.

Whether you believe in them or not, it is for you to decide.

It is five years since I got my first message, they continue to get my attention.

God speaks through His Messengers.

God has helped me in so many ways.

Someone was, and is, continuing to watch over me; I pray they always will.

During my career, I worked at various companies, which was no picnic I can tell you. Companies I worked for made me redundant four times in my career and I survived all of them. I worked for good companies and bad ones. It is all part of the territory in business, but we do tend to work usually for those with a good reputation.

I met wonderful people along the way. They certainly touched my life and I hope I touched theirs too.

What is amazing, is how time has flown. I am so glad that I can remember those times, the coma had no effect or distortion on my memory. In fact, it has enhanced it in so many ways.

Do you remember the old "Love is" saying?

"Love is all, Love is key, Love is everything..."

God has filled my life with love in so many ways.

God is Love; He lives in all of us.

We are never alone.

I feel so blessed after what He has done for me. God has saved my life twice in the last four years. That is amazing and remarkable.

It is not my time to go yet.

If love is the key, it has opened so many doors for me and it continues to do so. My life has been influenced by a lot of people in many ways.

I have recently returned 18th January 2019, back to Leeds General Infirmary. The Specialist Consultant told me officially of my hereditary genetic defect, which caused my Aortic valve to fail, although it had lasted a long time. It is amazing but true, and best of all, I am still here to tell my story.

The Specialist Consultant in Neuro Genetics said that I needed an MRI scan to check my condition and stretch of the valve, but this was only a formality.

As my consultant put it… "everything was done and dusted."

The "Gift" out of my coma is still firmly in control.

It is hard to explain, but there is a feeling of something else… a presence that was not there before. My Angel in white and female too, was there before me. My life has been changed by her presence and the very fact that I am still here, alive today.

I am very much aware of my fragility in all of this. I have been through everything in the last twelve months. The presence and feeling I have, has assured me, that my life is on course and that God is within me. It would be wrong for me to say that I am no longer afraid of dying or death. I have gained a kind of tolerance. Just how I will deal with all of that, still is a mystery.

I am sure that the "crossover" is not what we would expect, after my experience it will be far easier than we imagine.

I have recently read about angels in a book which says that St John did not describe them in more detail until The Book of Revelation, and what they look like, and their appearance.

In my second message in a dream, the words from The Book of Revelation were spoken by an Angel. All true I can assure you. I also read, angels only rarely appear, under extreme circumstances. They only make themselves visible to us then, and they can choose any form.

The "Gift" that came out of my coma is demanding in excellence and presence. There is no end to its achievements.

It is hard to describe, but I have a glowing type of feeling from within me that is full of confidence and potential. It does not accept failure or neglect. It feeds on success and continues to drive me on today.

My Gift is difficult to describe. I cannot challenge it. It is no use asking questions, as it thrives only on achieving the best way forward. My life has been changed by it all. An amazing Gift out of my coma.

Back in October 2018 I saw a Clairvoyant and she told me that my Spiritual Guide had crossed with me, could this explain it all?

It is incredible to know what I have done and all I have achieved in the last twelve months.

It is true when I say... my treasures are not of this World. There are no limits to their capabilities. Where this will all lead to in the future is a mystery. I know that more challenges lie ahead in the months and years before me. Whatever happened in my coma has changed me for the better. It has made my faith and beliefs deeper. I am lucky to have experienced all of this.

God has saved me.

I prayed to God and asked Him to.

God answered my prayers.

God could have taken me that day, instead He and the Surgeons saved me. I was reborn when I could have gone, at any time, from this World.

My light had gone out.

Now, it continues to burn brightly.

I feel as if I am a better person for what I have gone through.

I am convinced, this is only the start of things to come.

Optimism stems from every direction.

Love is the key and gift to it all.

CONTINUING SIGNS

My life has changed and there is no end with regards to the continuing messages and signs that are now, part of my life.

Recent messages are as follows... I recorded all these in my "storylines" book...

Saturday, 18th August 2018 (Note the date) Approximately 8:00 a.m. In a dream, just before waking... a man's soft voice.

"What would you do if God spoke to you through His messenger?"

4th September 2018. I found a piece of paper in my work jacket dated 8th August 2017, on it words I had written down from a desk calendar...

One loyal friend is worth ten thousand relatives.

WORDS OF WISDOM

It is what you do that defines who you are.

Believe in something, even if it means sacrificing everything.

Life is precious, it can disappear in a heartbeat.

5th September 2018. Music playing in a Charity shop as I enter... very spiritual and moving pop songs.

MORE CONTINUING SIGNS—MESSAGES
6th September 2018–01:54 a.m. Awaking from a dream.

Someone singing about "dispatches and the Lord is my

Shepherd."

Monday, 15th October 2018. I had a meeting with a Clairvoyant. I decided to see what they would make of my story of being in a coma, and what came out of it. I had never met her before.

This is what happened...

I had only just arrived at their door when they told me that my Mum was there...

"Your Mum says you had a good Surgeon, and that you are going to live a long time."

"What else does she say?"

"She says you must look after your heart and not to worry."

Amazing.

"She also says, your sister fought to the end with regards terminal cancer."

My sister died on 31st August 2018.

The Clairvoyant said that my sister was with my Mum but was so weak after trying to fight cancer. The Clairvoyant said that she would "gain sight" in about four months along with my Mum.

When I tell her of my messages and insight, she told me my Mum is laughing in the background.

My Mum knows the answer?

The Clairvoyant asks, "do I know a neighbour about 10–12 years ago, a tall man stooped?"

"I can't remember anyone like that" is my reply.

The Clairvoyant says that I have two guides. One being spiritual and another Guide in my life.

They are both watching over me.

When I tell her of the nurse in my coma who says "I am sorry you didn't make it, you are dead" she says it could be someone from another time, and that I too lived before, in another life.

When I ask about my dad, The Clairvoyant tells me he is on another level.

My Mum and my sister are on level 2, which is the closest to earth. My Mum says she will tell my dad of our meeting later.

The Clairvoyant says that Angels can assume any role... even appearing as a young nurse in my coma.

I was then given a full tarot reading by my Clairvoyant. She recommended taking care of my chest in December to January and informed something would happen with regards to my TV scripts in March 2019.

My Clairvoyant also confirmed that I had a "Gift" saying that my new talent could be improved by being in touch with other people. She recommended that attending classes would optimise that gift which would also help me to become a Spiritual Counsellor.

The meeting gave me the momentum to build on, knowing that my Mum is still watching over me, just as she promised in September 1987. The Clairvoyant said that her own gift was inherited from her grandmother when she was eighteen and that she had done spiritualism for over thirty-five years.

CONTINUING SPIRITUAL MESSAGES

Saturday, 20th October 2018. In a charity shop in Brighouse. A set of plates, large and small, my aunt had the same in her collection, now in my possession—on her

Welsh dresser.

Sunday, 21st October 2018. Approximately 8:30 p.m. The TV in front room… is ON! I had turned it off by remote.

Monday, 22nd October 2018. Approximately 1:10 a.m. Message in a dream…
A woman/young lady (very faint voice) saying "It's not over… there's a long way to go yet." I cannot remember the exact words, but this is how I remember the voice and their message.
I also remember a large building, an old co-op Victorian type building in green or blue woodwork, neon.
I do not know what this was saying.

Tuesday, 23rd October 2018. Approximately 9:15 p.m. On a Satellite TV channel in a well-known detective drama. The episode is "Atonement." A recently released unnamed prisoner is suspected of murdering a witness… Rob Cullen has been murdered and his daughter Mary Cullen was looking to avenge his death. The connection is in the names.

November 2018. On a certain TV channel, "Operation Live," uses the latest technology and with access to a London hospital, this three-part series follows life changing operations.
The opening episode captures open-heart surgery, from the moment the chest is opened by the Surgeons (like mine) and the heart is stopped, to when a valve is

then implanted and the heart restarts.

In a review the first episode informs full coverage of a surgical procedure *as it happens,* from an NHS trust in London. Surgeons guide viewers through open-heart surgery as they replace the aortic valve.

I just could not watch it.

Saturday, 24th November 2018. Approximately 7:40 p.m. Electric clock in bedroom flashing 12:59 p.m. All other in clocks ok. A coincidence or a warning?

Saturday, 15th December 2018. Approximately 3:40 p.m. Lights in house flashing. Strong electrical force. Turning off and dipping?

Tuesday, 25th December 2018. CHRISTMAS DAY. Approximately 16:10 p.m. Three lights flashing outside of back door.

CONTINUING CARE AT LEEDS GENERAL INFIRMARY

My recent medical procedure concerning replacement of my aorta valve in open-heart surgery, means that Doctors must monitor my aorta valve at my local Hospital and at Leeds General Infirmary. It's highly likely to be ongoing for the rest of my life. I must have Echo and MRI scans to check on my valve; whatever road I am on, it is unlikely I will ever get off, I take solace, in the fact, that I am still alive; I have not lost the knack of writing after completing the last five created dramas on my laptop. All of this keeps the brain alive.

What happened, whatever is inside me, they are the

one true influence, in all my actions now and I appreciate that most people will not understand. You must have been in a coma to know fully the implications. Like most people, I too did not know anything about comas. I had seen the odd film and documentary. Unless you have experienced being in a coma, it is not something you can explain.

All I can say is that there is a *satisfaction*, a feeling, call it what you will, something that was not there before. You feel changed, and in so many ways for the better. I feel a presence and guidance in everything I do and write. What I have is not of this World; I am not a superhuman and I do not have incredible strength. What I now have is a "heightening of the senses" an awareness and a form of "telepathy" all of which I am getting accustomed to.

My "Gift" is looking for success, which is loud and clear. It also controls the writing of all my books and TV scripts. It is quick to think of the next story to write. It's incredible really.

It is a fact that books take a long time to write. I can write a twelve-episode script in ten days and it's spontaneous. I write three pages in forty minutes, then conclude it the next day. I am always satisfied by this. I will have completed this accurately and with meaning. Fiction based on fact. Writing usually takes up to an hour a day. I then develop that into a sixty-page script for TV or film.

I have just written a drama, which may prove to be, the defining moment in my life. It is in three parts and called "The Saviour's Coming."

What I have written may turn out to be a significant

turning point for me. I have stuck to what is real and true; fiction does not actually work when you are writing about something incredible. I used specific evidence and supporting materials online to research my story.

I had drafted this three-part story in three days or approx. 4.5 to 6 hours. Another type of message, influenced my decision to write it…

This is what happened…

Sunday, 3rd February 2019. At 6.15am. Message/sign…

Our Catholic calendar fell to the floor in our dining room, this had never happened before. It revealed on the back these words…

"God made us a Family"

"We need one another, we love one another, we forgive one another, we work together, we worship together, together we use God's word, together we love all, together we serve our God, together we hope for heaven."

With that in mind, I began to draft my story.

DRAFTING AND WRITING MY STORY

I began by putting down the story lines for my new project. The next thing was to try and write "The Saviour's Coming."

I had an outline of something I had written from Christmas in my storylines book. I referred to this as part of writing my drama.

I had to create two central characters and if they worked well together, I would use them in future storylines; the story motivated me to write something that had not been done before. I am currently adapting the last two scripts... Christmas Angels (set in York) and The Saviour's Coming (set in New York), now that is a coincidence. I am in putting them on my laptop before I draft more stories. Most stories are handwritten.

I have other stories in the pipeline for the future.

I must write all my scripts by hand on A4 sheets of paper. Whoever my "Guardian angel" is they will only allow me to write using the *old* methods. I tried writing a script on my laptop, but it was as if everything had stopped. I had to go back to writing it in longhand, I now know, that it only favours the old traditional writing methods. I do not know who they are, but all the stories just continue to flow. How long will this last, probably until I can write no more. There is no end in sight.

Two or three of my scripts are returning series. All I need now is a Production company to take notice, I pray this will happen soon. If it is meant to be, it is meant to be, as the saying goes. You have got to keep going, keep believing. God is leading me on a road and challenges lie ahead. Where I am going, I do not know.

So many questions and somehow, I must fill in the blanks and find answers.

I am on an adventure. Who knows where all my writing will take me, everything is a blank canvas? Somehow, something tells me good things will happen, along the way.

The "Gift" out of my coma always seems to be in charge. It writes at speed. I never have writer's block; that never happens. Nothing is written twice or duplicate stories.

I have checked, all the thirty-three brand new episodes of The Persuaders. They are all different and original, not one of them is a duplication. They are set on the French and Italian Riviera's with the odd one in Venice, Milan, Lake Garda, Rome, and the UK.

I have been to the Italian Riviera numerous times over the years. The scenery is amazing with wonderful countryside, grape vines, olives, and magnificent roadways through the mountains. Monaco, Monte Carlo alongside Nice and Cannes on the French Riviera are beautiful places to visit; they are the inspiration for my series and the true stars of the show.

In contrast to my writing, it is now exactly a year, 16th February 2019, since my admission to hospital and Leeds General Infirmary in March. My scar from my neck to midriff is slowly fading, of course the actual experience will never fade, but things are getting better.

Now feeling rejuvenated and happy, in fact so happy to be alive, my writing has taken on another project. I wrote about angels and God in my last two series. I'm currently writing a series called The Champions that was first shown on TV in the late 1960s. It is over fifty-two years since it was on television. It is a science fiction type of story. I am writing a series of twelve episodes, my first story being "Reawakening."

The blank canvas has begun all over again.

I have already decided on the episode titles, now all I need do is draft the stories around them.

The internet is the perfect place to find details of locations, hotels, and situations which I adapt, it gives authenticity to all my writing. I do not particularly write in sequence.

I look at my title then write something around it, and it usually works.

So far, so good, these stories have again taken me on another journey. I never thought I would ever write fiction but "The Gift" does the rest and shows no sign of stopping.

More original created titles are emerging, as I write...

Thy will be done—One second from life, one second from death.

My brain is again in overdrive and continues to develop. Even now, a year on, the "Gift" out of my coma produces the most fantastic titles and stories. I guess it will continue, it's sheer belief of making it happen, continues daily.

It is a roller coaster ride now.

Whether success is around the corner or not, I have done everything that came out of my coma, all I need is luck to make it happen. I am open to everything and whatever happens in the future will be for the best, so they say.

Back in the Seventies everything was sophisticated. I remember going to Peter Stringfellow's Cinderella's in Leeds. Now that really was the height of sophistication, all "cut glass and corduroys" to quote a friend back then. It was an expensive place to go for dancing.

My faith continues to shine brightly and is my constant companion throughout my life. I am proud of what I have done and achieved. My hope is that I will continue to grow and mature in the future.

More ideas spring to mind concerning my writing.

My next story will continue where The Saviour's Coming left off, except this time it will be about the ten plagues of Egypt in a modern-day setting.

What is happening? This is not me, but another revelation of the coma and "Gift" that I now seem to have. Again, I have no idea how I am going to write it but no doubt my "Gift" does.

It will be another roller-coaster journey that is for sure.

I have now completed my twelve-part brand new series of The Champions. The stories are a world away from the original, but I have remained true to the characters and plots which have scripts relevant for today.

The Gift out of my coma shows no sign of slowing down. Now, anything Biblical is on the radar. I have just completed (1st April 20) a four-part drama called "Thy Will be Done." This is the title of my ten plagues of Egypt series. The story is amazing.

The Internet, whilst it has its downside, is a wonderful tool and inspires all my research for my stories. Everyone loves a good story, which is key to everything.

LOOKING AFTER MY HEART

I have recently returned to Leeds General Infirmary (5th April 2019) for an MRI scan. It is all part of the after care for my metal aortic valve replacement.

I think it would not be good for people who suffer with claustrophobia. You are asked to remove all clothing, wear a hospital gown, then to lay down on a table which transports you into the tunnel of the round MRI scanner. There are only three of these machines in Leeds. You then undergo a series of breathing in and out tests, having to *hold your breath* when the American Lady tells you on the headphones. What follows are loud banging sounds, it is all part of the procedure. You must endure this for fifty minutes.

The redeeming quality is they *piped* music to you through the headphones, mine being Eighties songs and they do take your mind off things. I was not alone in there either. The tunnel is full of lights, and it attracts various insects, in my case a red spider. They are supposed to be lucky. It was to the right of my forehead; it held its position throughout my scan. I hope it was lucky in my case.

You also have a square piece of electrical apparatus across your chest and electrodes around your heart. My consultant advised this was to check the mild situation of the elasticity of the aortic valve. It would need MRI scans on a regular basis at twelve-monthly intervals; all down to the aftercare after having major open-heart surgery.

My warfarin measurement had increased to 4mg (target 2.5 to 3.0) for no reason. Increases and decreases in medication happens often. It is all a question of the finding the right balance.

Modern medicine is always advancing.

Sunday, 7th April 2019. Visual.

A bowl of pears... one had a figure 3 on the outer skin. A lucky omen? I have photographic evidence on my mobile.

Angel number 3 played a part in my life. I had lived at a number 3 address then 111 at another house, in my early years. I checked on the Internet, and it advised... seeing the number 3 means you are in a creative situation. It also said that you would have a powerful need to express feelings, ideas, and visions of the imagination, quite true in my case.

I have now adapted my first fifty-page TV script, being an episode from "It's a kind of Love." This is my prototype called "No man is an Island." I must finely tune the story and add "laugh" lines. This is a comedy drama in twelve parts set in Leeds from 1987 to 1991. I have recently approached a Production Company and await the outcome of my writing. Now I am beginning to wonder if everything that has happened with regards my writing, is symbolically linked to me? So far, I have written about Angels... The Second Coming... The Ten plagues of Egypt. Now I am due to write about Mary Magdalene, all of which I would never have written about, had the coma not happened, or the "Gift" out of it. That is where I am now. It is Tuesday the 4th Holy week, Easter 2019. My subconscious tells me that it is no use looking for scientific answers, there are not any anywhere. All I can add is that for reasons unknown, my "Gift" is the revelation to everything.

I am now writing my new drama, The Magdalene Mystery. I have begun to draft my story. It is set in Cambridge and Oxford. This is what they now call a "crossover" series. Characters from another drama ending up in a current drama.

The drama begins when The Police find two bodies in Oxford and Cambridge at the same time. When cryptic clues are noticed by The Police on a grey slab they are baffled. I have done my homework, and everything is coming together nicely. It helps when you have visited the places in question, they call it "on location" in writing terms.

However, by clear strange reason there happens to be an incredibly old college in Cambridge called "Magdalene." I never knew anything about that at all. This now asks the question has the "Gift" out of my coma led me to this? Just as I have written in the opening it defines human logic.

I am using cryptic clues. There are so many conspiracy theories. In my crossover version... Nicola (from Angels Eyes and Christmas Angels) is in fact Mary of Bethany. Nicola will be revealed in the storylines that she is Mary Magdalene, a disciple and follower of Jesus.

Music still inspires me and always will. It has been a major influence in four or five of my dramas and writing. My twelve-part comedy drama "It's a kind of Love" has Eighties music running through it. Writing it has exceeded all my expectations; it's teeming with music. The story is based on my own original experience at a singles club in Leeds. They were wonderful years. I met so many lovely people and it helped me stage a couple of Telethons in the early Nineties. I also ran my own discos and events for over five years. A world away from today's internet and speed dating. It was quite a unique time when people genuinely met others in a comparable situation be it at a bar night or party. My writing continues to develop. Will it ever end? I do not know the answer to that question. All I can say is that it is quite demanding, concise, and precise in detail. My rollercoaster ride continues, there is no stopping this ride.

It's destiny calling... a power I dare not deny. Where destiny will lead me is not known but my incredible journey is ever changing. My privacy and health are especially important to me.

My twelve-part drama "It's a kind of Love," has inspired me to write a second series—set in 1992. My comedy drama is firmly set in Leeds and a national Telethon. ITV Telethon inspired me which was run by our local TV company; I put on countless events throughout the year to raise funds.

There is no magical formula to writing any of my dramas or comedy drama series. The inspiration for them all is straight out of "My Gift." If there was a magical formula, I would market and sell it.

You cannot see it, you cannot feel it, but it is within me, and no doubt always will be from now on. It is a strange thing to say, but if I do not write it gets *restless*. When it comes to drafting stories, I now have ways to finish them... no matter how complex. The "Gift" does not allow unfinished work at all. When I start writing I must complete it within the time allowed. After that it is on to the next one.

With regards to ITV Telethon '92 I had help when putting on major events.

My friend Bob asks,

"What about putting on a truck-pulling event in the main arena at Harewood House?" So, we put our idea forward to the local TV station asking if we could do it. They were full of praise for the event and said they would ask a "celebrity team" to take part against our club. This will be the icing on the cake. I told Bob of their decision and the next thing he advises is that he has organised two cab units for the event in July 1992. We are one of the events in the main arena.

Harewood House is a large country house on the outskirts of Leeds. It was built between 1759 and 1771. There are 120 acres of gardens and lakeside walks. It was the perfect place to stage the event.

I have become something of a "celebrity" myself at the club. I seem to have gained in stature when "putting on a show."

They of course have terrific taste.

The event at Harewood House was a fantastic success.

Telethons are wonderful fund-raising events. We raised over £2,636 in a series of events which ran for over six months. We presented our large cheque to a Yorkshire "Calendar" TV presenter. An air display by the red arrows followed. It was a wonderful sight.

It was a very satisfying end to a very worthwhile cause.

The end to what was a very perfect day. We were all left on a high.

I had become a veteran of putting on large events with Telethon '90 and Telethon '92 under my belt.

These too were all part of "The Gift" that I never knew I had. Everything seemed to fall into place, and everyone played their part. This was never just a "one man" show.

The best was yet to come.

SIGNS IN NUMBERS

Friday, 17th May 2019.   3.33am. The time on bedroom digital clock.

What does it mean? In Biblical terms 333 is significant. We believe that Jesus died at the age of thirty-three and the Holy Trinity equals three. As Catholics we believe that God is in three persons. God the Father, God the Son, and God the Holy Ghost.

When you multiply by three times it equals nine which signifies the word "completion" in numerology studies— 333 signifies a connection with spirit guides and ascended matters or ascended masters Jesus and Moses.

When you see the number 333 help and assistance is on the way. It can also signify truth and that we are all one. All things are equal but may not come to true potential as a human being. Number 3 also identifies as past, present, and future.

333 meaning—You have insight and are ready.

Ready for what?

There is no doubt that 333 is a powerful sign and message from the spirit.

Three is also the number of The Trinity and reminds us of "oneness" and the link between mind, body, and spirit.

All of this is incredible to me. There is no doubt, I am on a journey in life. The "Gift" I received out of my coma is strong. You cannot see it, feel it, or touch it. It is ever present, giving all, it must give in a creative sense. There is no time limit, I seem to have developed, and I am growing from it.

I know I am not alone, and that God really loves me.

I am still afraid of dying, the human side of me always will be, but God has saved my life and I am so grateful. Human frailty and weakness are something we all have. Our bodies are for a lifetime, but they too become weak and tired. We need to use all our strength to survive.

The latest revelation of 333 gives me complete control over everything to come. As I was *halfway between* worlds in my coma I realised that the crossover is just that, not like the life and death situation that we are all led to believe. Even though I have been privileged to see that, I am still afraid to let go of the here and now.

Human frailty is not the head of my existence. God is.

Monday, 25th September 2019. Approximately 10:00 a.m. At a local supermarket...

I tried on headphones. The song playing was... "Hello from the other side." No explanation.

Devine intervention. Devine protection?

Tuesday, 21st May 2019. At 3:33 a.m. I let our cat out and noticed the time. An hour later I let him in, it is now 4.44am. I have read this is one of a sequence of numbers designed to get your attention... it also serves as a "wake up" call from your spiritual guide.

444 like 333, is a powerful number. It means your angels are by your side and want the absolute best for you. They ask that you pay attention very carefully to the signs that you see around you, 444 is about understanding. It also reflects that something important has happened in your life which needs understanding?

Wednesday, 22nd May 2019. At 11:11 p.m. Time on mobile phone…

This is also a symbol of "spiritual awakening" supplying opportunities to determine what your purpose in life is. It also signals a time when you will start to feel more confident, independent, and motivated.

This number also signifies that your thoughts are becoming real. A spiritual presence is with you. The Divine is crossing your path and has a message to share, an assurance or acknowledgement of the present state of perfection.

INTERPRETATION OF NUMBERS

We are asked in numerology to take note of our actions, showing that you are on the right path. A presence is telling you the word "accept." A new time is beginning or ending. Something on your mind you see as a gift to yourself is making way to become real.

Saturday, 25th May 2019. 222 and 777 seen on car number plates.

222 has a spiritual meaning. It signifies a call to action, to further the path I am on or any new path I take. It also symbolises you have taken the actions of other people and recognise them as well.

You are in the right place at the right time.

Trust and stay focused on what you want, rather than what you do not want.

Everything is working out, according to the Devine, for the greater good. This number is also a reminder to keep the faith, stay true to what is about to happen. 777

stands for holiness. My guides are sending a message that it is ok to let fear go. It is a spiritual healing. Spiritual guides are with you when you see this number. Ask them for strength and courage. Allow your guides to surround you with love.

Thursday, 30th May 2019. 3:33 a.m. On Kitchen cooker clock.

Saturday, 1st June 2019. 3:33 a.m. As above.

Saturday, 1st June 2019. Approximately 7:25 p.m. Returning from mass. Car registration EEE, inside mirror reflects as 333.

Sunday, 2nd June 2019. In a dream.
I returned to my first home, number 3. My sister was in the ruins, I heard voices on site. We left in 1964.

Tuesday, 4th June 2019. 5:20 p.m.
We had significant thunderstorms early evening and the rain was pouring down.
I arranged to meet my partner at the bus stop at the bottom of the road.
I jumped in the car; the rain was really coming down. I started to negate the roads out of the estate, suddenly the car satellite seemed to malfunction.
A series of numbers 222 and 2222 started repeating all over the screen followed by "sa." The rain was interfering with the satellite.

Wednesday, 5th June 2019. I saw 777 on a car number plate at 11am.

Wednesday, 5th June 2019. Approximately 15:45 p.m. In a dream.

I was at my sister's house. I said that I had tried to tell her years ago, but she would not listen. My Mum was there. I tried to drive away in my car, but there were people all over the road. It was as if they had all been left behind.

I investigated into the meaning of "sa." It stands medically for sinoatrial, referring to one of the major elements in the cardiac conjunction system which controls the heart rate. It generates electrical impulses and conducts them throughout the muscle of the heart. It stimulates the heart to contract and pump blood. Third degree heart block is congenial where the condition is present "at birth."

According to medical terms, deaths that are caused under these conditions are VERY RARE.

Another omen?

Thursday, 6th June 2019. Approximately 9:40 a.m.
Two collared doves flew in front of my car when driving down the road.

Is this another sign from Heaven?

The symbolism of seeing a pair of doves is immensely powerful. It is even more powerful when you see them in front of you, they symbolise fidelity and love.

My next writing project will be "The Power and the

Glory." A three-part story about Aztecs, The Vatican catacombs, and their links?

I have called my second drama "Signs from Heaven." I have based this drama on all the numbers and electrical signs, questioning what it all means.

The "Gift" out of my coma, still shows no sign of ending.

Tuesday, 11th June 2019. Approximately 1:00 a.m. A thought was *put* inside my mind.

...*All who are on the side of truth hear my voice.*

Jesus spoke these words in front of Pilate on Good Friday.

Truth is the foundation of everything good in our lives. What we accept as true becomes a principle that governs our lives.

Here is the truth. Your soul is priceless. It makes up who you are. It is the eternal you. Our bodies are temporary, but your soul is forever.

Sunday, 16th June 2019. Approximately 10:45 a.m. A simple prayer book had fallen from a shelf. It landed on pages 58–59, inside were the following words...

"I believe in The Holy Spirit, the Lord, the giver of life who proceeds from the Father and the Son who with the Father and The Son is adored and glorified, who has spoken through the prophets."

"I believe in one, holy, Catholic apostolic Church. I confess one baptism for the forgiveness of sins. I look forward to the resurrection of the dead and the life of the World to come. Amen."

Friday, 28ᵗʰ June 2019. Approximately 10:30 a.m. I played a CD and checked the running time of the track, it read 3.33 minutes.

Saturday, 29ᵗʰ June 2019. 3:33 a.m. Time noticed, on digital clock in bedroom.

Monday, 1ˢᵗ July 2019. Approximately 10:30 a.m. 555. I saw this on a car number plate at my local supermarket.

555 is a powerful number. It stands for the wholeness of creation. It is the number of Christ, countless unities, in consciousness, it is symbolic and Biblical.

The significance of numbers continues throughout the year and are still in evidence today.

GUARDIAN ANGELS ARE PRESENT

Today, Friday 19th July 2019 I returned to Leeds General Infirmary to see my Cardiology Consultant. I had my yearly MRI scan and The Consultant updated me with regards my mechanical aorta valve. Everything was as it should be with no cause for alarm for the future.

Signs and messages continue in numbers. I find them comforting.

Saturday, 27th September 2019. A poster outside a local church it read...

"It is better to walk alone in the right direction than to walk with others in the wrong direction."

Returning to Cardiology was a strange experience for me. I thought I would be happy with joy at my return, considering all the love I have for them. Instead, I had a different feeling altogether. I felt nothing at all when I visited there. A strange feeling. I could not understand why I felt this way. I realised sometime later that I was going back to where my coma and drama took place concerning my life, yet I felt nothing. What is wrong with me? It was as if, someone was saying "I got you out of hospital, why have you brought me back here?"

I returned from holiday in Italy on 25th September 2019 but I was having a problem concerning my urine. It was "pinking." I phoned the Warfarin clinic and they suggested I reduce my dose to 3mg; the Nurses said reducing the dosage would bring down the measurement and back to normal. I asked if there was a problem. The nurses informed me that it could be an infection. I returned to my local hospital on Monday, 30th September 2019 and saw my consultant. He said it was down to a change of dosage concerning my warfarin. It was very upsetting to see this; all sorts of things run through your mind. Yet another thing I must endure on my continuing journey. Life does not prepare you for all the twists and turns that come your way.

As a friend recently said to me, "it's no fun getting old, is it?"

They are right.

I am just starting to write my eighteenth TV drama. Yes eighteen. Amazing but true. I call it "Document of Truth" and it tells the story of a "hidden text" within in a book by Galileo. This cannot be me, someone else must be writing it. There is so much content and information, it is also complex.

My script will be to write it based on fact, which is, a very tall order. I am aiming to tell this story in three episodes. It is another title and story straight out of my coma.

Whatever is happening I am on a kind of journey. The dramas are merely diversions to get the message across.

What next? I do not know.

In this book I am recording all the facts that are now relating to sequence of numbers in my life. Someone told me on holiday that I was a "special person" because of the trauma and my coma experience. There could be truth in that.

With regards my waterworks, hopefully after five days

I am now clear…

Thursday, 26ᵗʰ to Monday 30ᵗʰ June 2019, I am clear. Clear from 1ˢᵗ October 2019. Five days.

Wednesday, 2ⁿᵈ October 2019. My Warfarin reading taken in my finger reads 2.4. This is a dramatic fall from 4.6 and 4.2. All of this has something to do with seeing 555 and 333.

The Warfarin Clinic Nurses were baffled by the sudden change, so am I. Everything is now back to normal.

Was it really an infection or something else?

Perhaps, Divine intervention has helped?

I am unlikely to find any answer in this World.

Friday, 11ᵗʰ October 2019. I revisited a Clairvoyant, a year to the date.

I was excited to find out what she would say. Would my books or TV scripts produce the results that I was looking for?

The Clairvoyant said that my Grandad was interested in me pursuing my writing. She also said my Mum was there too.

I had never met my Grandad. He died in the 1920s long before I was born. I asked if my Mum could remember where my birthmark was.

The Clairvoyant said her response was that it was on my right leg next to my knee. She was correct. Now I know this is for real!

I asked if my sister was with my Mum. The Clairvoyant told me she was on "another level." My Mum said she was doing another job.

My Clairvoyant said that my Mum is "all around me."

When I spoke about my recent visit to see the Consultant, at Leeds General Infirmary and the possibility of more surgery. The Clairvoyant advised my Mum said that it was "all talk" and "you know what doctors can be like."

I had a full spread tarot reading. The Clairvoyant recommended taking it easy in October. She also said November to February were exceptionally good months and there would be progress concerning my writing. No problems health wise at all. She advised to live normally; she could not see anything ahead.

The Clairvoyant said that my writing "came out of my coma" and is a "gift."

My Spiritual Guide continues to watch over me.

Saturday, 12th October 2019. 10:45 a.m. Car Reg in supermarket carpark 555 and in mobile number 777444.

Tuesday, 26th November 2019. Something very strange happened today. I had taken my car in for a service, to a car dealer in Leeds. I had left for the garage at 7:00 a.m. I returned home at 11:00 a.m. and felt tired after taking my medication. I had a nap and out of it came a strange dream. My recollection in that dream, which had blurred vision, I remember my Mum being there. I was putting my shoes into a briefcase or plastic bag. I am sure she told me to "wake up." The time was 16:50 p.m. I awoke to find my mobile advising of a new message. I received it at 16:51 p.m. from a London

Theatre Director and Producer. It was in response to my application for "It's a kind of Love" comedy drama. The words received were very inspiring... *"I would like to add that it was a pleasure to read your play, which was very inspiring. Do stay connected, as we will be having further productions in the future."*

A Clairvoyant predicted this in my tarot reading of 11th October 2019.

After lunch I wrote the second episode of my new drama "O Come, O Come, Emmanuel—The real Christmas 11th September 3BC."

Investigations so far, have taken me from the Vatican to Bethlehem and The Church of the Nativity, the birthplace of Jesus. A fourteen-pointed star marks the spot.

Whatever drives me to write like this comes from within and from the "Gift" I received out my coma in March 2018.

Something very strange happened today at the garage, I met a gentleman who had two pacemakers fitted at Leeds General Infirmary. Unlike me he was not in a coma and said he could only remember "darkness."

My Guardian Angels continue to send messages by numbers.

8th December 2019. I have today made a significant discovery and probable answer as to why I keep seeing 3 or 333.

There is no end in sight to my writing.

It continues and flourishes, no subject is off limits.

I recently had a visit from a certain party about the upcoming General Election. This is the end of November 2019. You know how it goes, you are trying to get your car into the garage, when suddenly someone said,

"Excuse me could you tell me which party you are going to vote for in December?" Obviously, I cannot say which party that was, but it gave me an idea.

I decided to write a comedy drama called "Get Brexit Done."

I had absolutely no intention of writing anything about Brexit, but this visit inspired me to put pen to paper. I used characters I had invented out of my "It's a kind of Love" series and it worked. I decided I would base it in West Yorkshire...

"Get Brexit Done"—This is how the story goes...

When Gez reunites with Mike in Mawfield, they hatch a plan in this six-part comedy drama, to bring Yorkshire folk together in a Brexit fight to the finish.

The Government throw a spanner in the works when they announce a General Election in December 2019... but they have no Tory candidate in Mawfield.

It is unbelievable that after three and a half years we are all stuck in the EU, even though four or five deals had been agreed.

Mike decides to stand as the Conservative party candidate... with Gez and Ernest as backup. Mike and Gez, recruit a couple of girls to help... The Brexit Rap is a winner... it goes viral Worldwide on the Internet.

Can they help Prime Minister Boris Johnson "Get Brexit Done" by beating Corbyn's Labour? The only problem is Mawfield has been a safe Labour seat for over seventy-five years. Can Mike change their minds by… talking the talk… walking the walk… and doing the Brexit Rap?

This is a Yorkshireman's take on it all.

If we were politicians… we would make mincemeat of them all.

We Yorkshire folk… tell it how it is… no beating about the bush.

17.4 million who voted for Brexit cannot be wrong.

Prepare for laugh aloud humour in this comedy take on all the political wrangling in Westminster and the European Union… with plenty of Yorkshire grit.

LET'S GET BREXIT DONE… ONCE AND FOR ALL.

It was a real pleasure and joy to write this drama. My characters came to life on the page from the Teaser to the last scene. It also has its own soundtrack which adds to the flavour of the writing and event.

"Get Brexit Done" became the twenty-fourth series out of the "gift" in my coma.

At the beginning of my writing, I decided to dramatize events with regards being in a coma.

Between 9th August 2018 to 3rd September 2018. I drafted my next story "IN A COMA." It is in twelve parts.

When it comes to writing for television, I usually take my four/six-page first episode and turn it into a sixty-page script adding more detail, story lines, and characters. It all pans out before my eyes.

This all comes naturally to me.

I will add that, when I decide to write my script, I must write another series alongside what I am doing; it is a formula I used and all part of the "Gift."

My explanation concerning the gift is that this is the price I must pay for still being alive; it is a small price to pay when life is so precious.

It is forever, evolving.

REBORN FOR A NEW GENERATION

In addition to all my dramas and comedy dramas, I have also written various classic TV series, with a modern plot and called them "Reborn for a New Generation."

I am talking about series that we all loved and grew up with. Four or five of them were filmed by various TV companies over fifty years ago, but they still pack a punch when shown today. I would say it was our "golden era" in television and that nothing can match it today.

What I usually do is, after writing a couple of drafts of my original and created dramas or comedy dramas, I write something relating to a classic drama from the past. Why? Just because I can do. Again, it is no effort on my part.

I am always amazed at what I have written.

Writing an updated version of The Persuaders, was straight out of my coma. I had watched it on a satellite channel in hospital before I had my operation. They had a profound impact on me.

This is the header I wrote, for the new series...

"Its unique mix of comedy, action, and spectacular scenery on the French and Italian Rivera's combine to make it an instant classic.

Lord Brett Sinclair... charming, debonair and an English aristocrat with Danny Wilde... American, witty, and outspoken... a self-made Millionaire... come together to defeat whoever gets in their way... guided by Judge Fulton and Italian aristocrat Countess Suzanna Minori... making an explosive persuasive force."

Inspired by watching the original series... and from

"The Gift" I received out of my coma in March 2018.

In this new thirty-three-part series set on The Continent and the UK... action adventure is guaranteed.

The Persuaders have truly been reborn.

It also comes with a soundtrack to match. Even the "Funky Chicken" dance is in the series.

In between other projects I wrote The Champions, a remake of a 1967 series brought up to date. It became number nine in my list of TV scripts, it is one of my favourites...

This updated version starts where our three main leads, Craig Stirling, Richard Barratt, and Sharron Macready are miraculously rescued after their plane crashes in a snow drift in Tibet, following a secret mission. When they awake... they realise they have received... special powers, superhuman strength, telepathy, and ESP... as well as an overall heightening of their natural senses.

In this new twelve-part version all three Agents are in operation as The Champions of Law, Order and Justice... Operators of the International Agency of NEMESIS...

Episode highlights are as follows...

When terrorists ambush Richard in the Austrian Alps... he must use all his superhuman skills to escape his assailants.

The Shard in London is taken over by terrorists during an attack... Nemesis assigns Craig, Sharron, and Richard to help British Intelligence in a rescue mission. Tremaine is captive.

In Operation Tibet, The Champions return looking for answers... what they find is the paradise of Shangri-la...

A commercial airliner on a flight from Geneva to New York runs into trouble and Craig must use all the powers at his disposal to bring the flight under control... but will it all go according to plan?

Another favourite to have a makeover was The Man from U.N.C.L.E. I remember this series well, from my college days. It did not come under the "Reborn" banner but had an impact all on its own... I drafted this drama in three parts between 8th October and 15th October 2019.

The Man from U.N.C.L.E–The Domination of the World Affair. It is set in The Cold War and The Swinging Sixties... The Man from U.N.C.L.E. meets The Girl from U.N.C.L.E. when an unknown organisation holds the World to ransom.

Stylish, sophisticated, full of Sixties charm and pizzazz... Enforcement Agents Napoleon Solo and Ilya Kuryakin return to stop a takeover of the World; U.N.C.L.E assign Solo and Kuryakin to investigate when their Chief... Alexander Waverley... goes missing at The United Nations Building in New York and must travel the globe when U.N.C.L.E. agent April Dancer disappears.

Are both disappearances linked?

Together with Mark Slate... Solo and Kuryakin must race against time to find them both before an unknown organisation subjects the World to a secret deadly formula—of mass destruction.

But who is the unknown organisation behind it all? Is a nasty little bird called T.H.R.U.S.H the brains of the operation? More classic series are to be drafted as my writing continues to develop.

THE WAY FORWARD

Messages continue in number form; just as they have done, throughout the year.

Wednesday, 18th December 2019. A phone call from the nurse at my local surgery says my potassium levels are ok in my last blood test. I asked my Mum to help me. Can you believe it?

It is amazing.

No further tests or appointments to see The Consultant at Leeds General Infirmary until next year. I have my annual MOT in December next year.

However, a Nurse informed me at my local surgery, about rising sugar levels. It is in everything we eat. She recommended cutting down on intake, as levels had risen to pre-diabetes status. What is next?

I did wonder when that might happen. The plan of action is to get back to what I used to eat during the day at work and to cut out sugary intake. This may help next time. Christmas this year is to be on a normal basis, but not as many mince pies!

Wednesday, 18th December 2019. Approximately 10:20 p.m. The light in the window of our front room dipped three of four times. It was as if a large object passed through. It lasted two or three minutes until switched off by auto control.

I checked the light over on Thursday and found that it had blown. This usually happens when something like this takes place. Whatever blew the light had lots of force.

Sunday, 22nd December 2019. BBC News. Catastrophic fires in Sydney, Australia. They were almost apocalyptic.

Monday, 23rd December 2019. Approximately 12:20 p.m. I was watching a Biblical epic on TV. It was at the part where Jesus was on trial with Pontius Pilate, when He spoke these words...

"He who ever believeth in me shall have eternal life."

The wreath on the front door was *knocking*. I thought someone was there. When I checked there was no one around. It was a windy day though.

More signs in numbers continue to the end of the year.

My Horoscope for 2020 is as follows...

"It is a big year for Capricorns. Not only do you begin 2020 with Saturn but over the year a great cosmic teacher has a major impact. Just because something has always been a certain way it does not mean it must stay that way."

"You will find responsible ways to restructure and reorganise things in your life. You will experience a new sense of ease."

"You sometimes find it hard to take a chance when there is no guarantee of success. Luck and optimism are in your sign for the entire year. If you seize opportunities as they arise, you will be surprised and pleased with the results."

"The solar eclipse in June encourages you to find the courage to set off into uncharted territory. This potentially holds treasure for you."

In another reading for Capricorn (my sign) it says

"good fortune" everywhere and that I could *"hardly wish for a positive start to the new decade. Enthusiasm in January propels you towards a prize goal that is on your horizon. The only potential hazard, in this positive cosmic climate, is that you grow so confident of success, that it may overwhelm you."*

Positive thoughts for 2020.

Bush fires continue to get out of control in Australia. They are heading towards Sydney. The fire is unstoppable; hundreds are heading towards the capital. This is no longer down to "climate change," it is much more than that. The sky has turned black, then blood red. They are now calling it "an act of God."

I remember the first message I had in April 2014 "Leave them to God."

New reports advise of more deaths and hundreds of homes in Australia have been confirmed destroyed by fire due to deadly bushfires. Terror and destruction are all consuming; it has become a challenge, extremely dangerous and out of control. Fires continue to rage. It is an unprecedented crisis. Meteorologists say no rainfall is expected in Australia for another month.

As Australia burns the rest of The World can only wait.

An act of God?

Monday, 6th January 2020. I was watching a medical film on a satellite channel. Whilst undergoing heart surgery a young man experiences INTRAOPERATIVE AWARENESS.

Was it part of what I was going through?

Messages in numbers continue to flourish throughout January.

Wednesday, 8th January 2020. I completed my latest drama in three parts.

Stigmata— "Bearing the wounds of The Christ."
This is a term used by members of the Catholic faith to describe body marks, sores, or sensations of pain in locations corresponding to the crucifixion wounds of Jesus Christ on the hands and feet, the lance wound at the side, the head wounds from the crown of thorns and the scourge wounds over the entire body, particularly the back.

Vatican officials become overwhelmed when victims of the Stigmata start to come forward from all over the World.

Cardinal Raphael assigns Monsignor Kevin O'Flaherty and Professor Brookstein to investigate into the global phenomenon to find out why so many people have been afflicted with stigmata by the wounds of Christ's suffering.

Claims are made by others that they have become Christ's messengers on earth and are asking for an audience with The Holy Father.

Max and The Monsignor travel to Florence to contact a priest who claims to have "divine powers of Levitation, Prophecy and Bilocation."

Afflictions of leprosy in three or four people have also been reported by The Vatican as a stigmatised infliction worldwide—with irreversible consequences.

When a young woman, Maria Stefani questions The Monsignor and Professor Bookstein, she also bears the stigmatised marks of The Christ but holds a message for The Holy Father.

A sequence of events take place.

The Vatican dispatch Max and The Monsignor to the Pyramid of Cestus on the outskirts of Rome.

Will ancient Roman frescoes hold the key to everything?

World Governments put everyone on alert by strange warnings in climate change...

Could this be the pre-warning of The Second Coming?

This was another challenge. My next project concerns the Shroud of Turin.

Every project is continuing to grow in strength.

These are things I could never have written about in the past.

Signs in numbers continue throughout the month. My books are full of these signs.

Thursday, 23rd January 2020. Approximately 12:15 a.m. A strange but real dream.

All the characters in my TV dramas came to life. Richard Barratt and Craig Stirling out of The Champions... at the end saying, "we'll all meet again in the future." Incredible but true.

Saturday, 25th January 2020. At 6.36am. Time on mobile phone. I checked on the internet, and it said when you see 636 you are connected by this to the realm of divine Guardian Angels.

Sunday, 26th January 2020. Approximately 8:25–8:30 p.m. Interference going through a DVD. When I played it again there was nothing on the disc? There are two or three of comings and goings; it was as if someone was trying to speak through the TV. All very strange.

Monday, 27th January 2020. At 6:06 a.m. A song with a strong message playing on the radio.
Is someone trying to tell me something?

A NEW DECADE

After writing my four-part drama about Stigmata I decided to write something completely different to start 2020.

It's my six-part drama called "Adam Adamant Lives!" Another one of my "reborn" stories. The classic series was last broadcast on TV in 1966. I had always loved it. I decided to give it a 2020 remake.

"Adam Adamant Lives!"—This is how it all unfolds...

When Edwardian Adventurer, Adam Adamant, attends a gala evening in 1900s London, he is led into a trap by his arch nemesis "The Face" ... he then vanishes and is condemned to a living death.

"So clever... but oh so vulnerable."

In 1966 demolition workers find him below a Victorian building... still alive, frozen in a block of ice. They take him to hospital and after doctors discharge him, he finds that he is in a vastly different World... intact and unaged.

Adam has countless adventures in modern day Britain... but unbeknown to Adam "The Face" pursues him... having also regenerated in the Swinging Sixties.

Adam falls into his trap again and lies unfound for another fifty-four years in a rapidly dissolving ice block below the Elizabeth Tube line in London 2020. Surveyors discover him and they quickly transport the block to hospital where Doctors revive him, unscathed, just in time.

When MI6 investigate his story and track him down, they begin another chapter in the Adventurers life by reinventing him to solve crimes and evils... in this unpredictable century.

When Adam comes round in hospital, he meets Gabrielle Jones, one of the Surveyors who came to his rescue.

"I'm indebted to you dear lady, for saving my life. Please tell me where I am, and what year is it?"

"I'm Gabrielle Jones, one of the Surveyors working on the new Elizabeth Line. You're in London."

"And what year is it?"

"2020."

"My God... 2020... it can't be! Did you say your name was Jones? I don't suppose you know Miss Georgina Jones, do you?"

"She's, my Mum."

...and so, Adam reunites with Georgina whom he met in 1966 and the adventures begin all over again in 2020. I wrote those six episodes from 13th January to 23rd January 2020, writing for only an hour each day, weekends off.

My visions in numbers continue throughout January, as they do today.

Monday, 3rd February 2020. Approximately 12:15 a.m. I woke from a strange dream. I remember shouting "get out." I asked my partner— she said she heard nothing; these words came into my head...

THE FORGIVENESS OF SINS.

Friday, 7th February 2020. At 14:41 p.m. The time on Cooker clock.

I investigated this number; it means that one is blessed with the ability to regenerate and rise above any problems.

Incredible but true.

Wednesday, 12th February 2020. Approximately 8:00 p.m. The cross in the kitchen fell with a miraculous medal... it read... "At the Blessed Grotto I have prayed for you. Our Lady of Lourdes."

This was very strange as it had stayed in place for nineteen years! Was someone trying to tell me something?

More messages in numbers continue throughout February.

My next drama (Number 28) is... "Countdown to the end of time." I have written four episodes. It took less than nine days to complete, in hourly segments.

"Countdown to the end of time."—The synopsis is as follows...

A real Doomsday clock exists... as a symbol that stands for the likelihood of a manufactured catastrophe.

Today in 2020, it is set at one hundred seconds to Midnight which makes it closer than ever before in our planet's history.

Is it the end of the World? Is the World on the brink of nuclear annihilation and now climate change dominates the Earth... out of control?

As the potentially lethal Coronavirus spreads

Worldwide... Governments enforce lockdown in major cities. Travel restrictions are in place... and the death toll continues to rise.

As the crisis begins governments confirm there are millions of people affected all over the World. It has now spread to Japan and The United States of America... with cases reported in Scotland.

A meeting of COBRA is taking place in the UK.

Professor "Max" Brookstein requests the help of Monsignor Kevin O'Flaherty of The Vatican when The President asks them to search for answers with all other World scientists.

The World admits those answers... may be hard to find. This is a very real story that is happening today.

We are advised... although this is a Worldwide concern the chance of catching it is low... but is this to stop the panic?

Is it a cover up?

Meanwhile, swarms of locusts are covering Africa ...

ARE THESE THE SIGNS OF THE SECOND COMING AND ARMAGEDDON? IS THIS REALLY THE END OF TIME?

A stark warning and reminder of what the World was going through in early 2020.

Thursday, 13th February 2020. Approximately 11:15 a.m. Armed Police in black 4x4 BMW near shops in the centre of town. This is the kind of World we live in now.

Friday, 21st February 2020. Approximately 1:11 a.m. In a dream.

I remember asking my Guardian Angels in my prayers to be with me, then I had the weirdest of dreams...

It was something out of The Champions. My form of telepathy was in contact with someone on the other side.

I investigated the number 111. It symbolises the principles of spiritual awakening, enlightenment, high energy, inspiration, intuition, self-expression, and sensitivity.

Friday, 21st February 2020. I had reached a milestone concerning my writing.

I am about to write my thirtieth drama. It is over two years since I had major open-heart surgery at Leeds General Infirmary. As it is such a milestone, I have decided to write something with meaning. My new drama being "Save Us, Saviour of the World."

It is about the Turin Shroud and another of THE VATICAN MONSIGNOR stories. It deals with new evidence pointing the way to details of The Second Coming. I could never have written such dramas in the past. I just would have had no idea where to start. Now it is all mandatory, I just do not know when to stop. "My Gift" keeps evolving. Am I controlling it, or is it controlling me?

Tuesday, 25th February 2020. Approximately 6:25 p.m. Checked mobile.

I've used 444mb to date. I was checking on details for the End of the World—Coronavirus—Ash Wednesday. THE BOOK OF REVELATION (my second, spoken message in 2014) is linked to the end of the World and Armageddon.

My TV script writing goes from strength to strength. I have just entered "Get Brexit Done" Episode One—We're right behind you... to the BBC and following that up with a drama for ITV called "Sky High" which is set on the French and Italian Riviera. This is my "pilot" episode. It has a wonderful setting with amazing locations, Monaco, Monte Carlo, Cannes and Nice. They are wonderful places. I have been there countless times when visiting the area.

I previously entered Angel Eyes—Between the Living and the Dead. This drama is set in Leeds and York.

As I write my current drama, "Save Us, Saviour of The World" I am also looking to the future, I have decided to write "Ash Wednesday" which looks for answers concerning the recent coronavirus outbreak.

Italy currently has eleven towns in the Lombardy and Northern regions in lockdown. Hopefully in six months' time we will be able to travel on our holiday to Diano Marina.

Will it all be over by then?

26th February 2020. Today is Ash Wednesday, the time on the digital clock in our bedroom says 5:55 a.m. As with every Ash Wednesday, it is a day of fast and abstinence, no meat today. We also fast on Good Friday but that is six weeks ahead.

Thursday, 27th February 2020. Approximately between 2:30–4:30am. In a dream...

My Mum asked me to print names on a piece of

paper… I can remember two—Ruth Schofield and Joe Farrar. She said they were in the next room. Both had died decades ago.

Thursday, 27th February 2020. Time on Laptop 09:09 a.m.

Angel number 909 is a sign that changes are coming. You must embrace these changes and have faith in them because these momentous changes, are blessings from God.

More visual messages continue into March.

Wednesday, 4th March 2020. Approximately 1:20 a.m. I am waiting for our cat "angel Tom" to come back in. As I wait, I have the TV on for company. Nothing on really except a channel showing regional ghost stories. I note the name of the pub. It is not one I am familiar with, although I do visit the area to see my Osteopath, as and when needed.

In this pub, a naughty ghost is present. As things begin to happen, all sorts of objects are flying around the room. The crew used a "special word" and an analysis machine.

When they asked their name, the response was "death." When they asked, "what do you want us to do," the response was "die." I felt sick inside. Was it my "spiritual guide" responding?

My "spiritual guide" is of the light, and they walk in the light. I really felt strange for a while, all of this was down to the horrible encounter with viewing this on TV.

Monday, 9th March 2020. Approximately 7:00 p.m. I

checked online for the first time...

Q. What is the name of the angel who helps or guides me to write, or who is it that writes through me?
A. ARCHANGEL GABRIEL

Archangel Gabriel is the Messenger Angel, who collaborates with writers and all communicators. He is also associated with creative writing. Unbelievable, after two years to the day when I had major open-heart surgery, and the "Gift" I received out of it, I now know the name of who it is that drives me on. I have taken boundaries I would never have taken or written, had it not been for their guidance.

I have written and completed thirty-one series to date, comprising of 12,6,4 or 3-parts.

It is still all incredible to me. If publishers recognise my work, it will be an amazing achievement, all out of my coma. Even if it does not happen, the very fact that I have written thousands of words is just unreal, that alone is a fantastic personal achievement.

Archangel Gabriel is known as the "angel of revelation" or "announcement." He plays a significant role in Christianity acting as a Messenger for God.

September. 2017. In a dream...
A young girl and her mother saying, "who do you think you are?"

Suddenly another voice "Wonderful Counsellor... I am His Messenger."

Gabriel is a seraph of The Holy Angels who acts as a

messenger. He is known as Saint Gabriel the Archangel, with Archangel in the sense of capital "A" as in Prince of Angels, not as in class of angels who are just above the "normal angels" (guardian angels).

Gabriel is one of the Seven Archangels.

He is one of the most well-known angels. Gabriel is known as the angel who reached out to Mary before the virgin birth...

"Do not be afraid Mary, for you have found great favour with God. You will give birth to a son, and you will call him Jesus. The Saviour."

The Bible states that the prophecy is complete. In a dream I heard the words "Wonderful Counsellor" in September 2017. I decided to investigate why I heard it spoken then and not in December.

I found out; the actual birth date of The Christ was 11th September 3BC. This would tie in with the message from Gabriel at the end of September!

Messages continue to flourish throughout March.

I have written thirteen dramas to date out of my coma concerning The Second Coming or events leading up to it. All of these began in January 2019.

Saturday, 14th March 2020. Europe is now the "epicentre" of the deadly coronavirus.

Can all of this really be happening in modern day 2020?

The answer is yes! All we can do is wait, and as it says in The Bible "hope that it passes us by."

ASH WEDNESDAY AND THE CORONAVIRUS

I have now completed my next project "Ash Wednesday" which is in four parts.

"Ash Wednesday"—The story is as follows...

When evidence appears that the deadly coronavirus plague, predicted in The Bible, claims begin to appear that the end of the World is near.

In this very current drama, the chain of events confirms over 77,000 cases have developed in China with more than 2,663 deaths. As the virus spreads to Europe and the rest of the World with cases rising, Governments begin to stop further contamination.

Scientists predict that we are on course for a pandemic which may eventually change into a Worldwide epidemic.

With no vaccine to counteract the virus The Vatican sends Monsignor Kevin O'Flaherty to meet Professor "Max" Brookstein in Milan, which is in lockdown. Together they work with World Scientists for a cure in hope of stopping the deepening crisis and global emergency.

Back in December 2014 in a dream, I heard the words "The Book of Revelation." I did not know what it meant then. I thought it might have been a warning. The Book of Revelation speaks of Angels and prophecies leading up to the end of the World.

The World needs an antidote... but will one be found by World Scientists, and just how much time have we got left?

REMEMBER THOU ART DUST... AND TO DUST YOU WILL RETURN

ASHES TO ASHES... DUST TO DUST

I wrote all of this on 13th March 2020, prior to lockdown in the UK.

This is my thirty-first drama series and tells of the outbreak, of the now very real and current coronavirus on a Worldwide scale.

As I write all of Italy is now in total lockdown.

The Coronavirus plague was predicted in The Bible long ago.

Earthquakes, flooding, forests burning in six or more countries together with famines are all cause for concern.

Why is all of this happening?

Tuesday, 10th March 2020. Coronavirus update–116,871 cases and 4,095 deaths Worldwide.

The virus is also known as COVID-19.

In the UK there are 373 cases and six deaths to date. We are on the brink, of a national emergency pandemic.

Coronavirus knows no boundary or border. Stock markets Worldwide are plunging... massive areas of The World now affected. Can all of this be happening in 2020?

Scientists say no known cure has been found anywhere to date. In addition to the Coronavirus large swarms of locusts are now present in certain parts of the World.

Messages through numbers continue to flourish.

Tuesday, 17th March 2020. HAPPY ST. PATRICK'S DAY.

Today, everything is far from happy. We are in the grip of the coronavirus, and it ranks as the worst disease on the planet. Every country is affected and in lockdown. It has spread and become profoundly serious in the last six weeks. All normal activities, everything we have known has all swept away, lives lost, lives changed. Devastation Worldwide. This is no Hollywood blockbuster.

This really is reality and happening today!

As of 14th March 2020 there has been more than 144,078 cases and 5,397 deaths Worldwide.

Conspiracy theories are rife now. The official story is that "the virus" came from a market in Wuhan, China.

We are all under threat as the deadly Covid-19 goes from strength to strength.

A vaccine or antidote may be months or years away.

The World Health Organisation have declared it to be a "global emergency" and a pandemic.

Italy is hardest hit, so far, with over 17,000 cases and 1,266 deaths to date.

The Government are recommending that we isolate, keep away from other people and gatherings, and to stay indoors for fourteen days if we get it. Could it be the end of the World? Is 2020 the year when the Apocalypse takes place?

No one knows.

"Be ready... for you will not know the day or the hour, when I will return" as it says in The Bible.

I never thought I would ever write about such things in any of my books or TV scripts... yet I have done.

When I first wrote of "The Saviour's Coming" in January 2019, was I actually writing about the chain of events or my "spiritual guide?"

Was it a premonition of what was to come?

Churches are all closing too because of contact with others.

We are all heading for lockdown.

Tuesday, 17th March 2020. The Prime Minister advised on all TV channels that "the UK is on a war footing" this has never happened since World War 2.

All fifty states in America have Covid-19.

We are all "under attack" from an unseen enemy. It has dealt a blow that could kill tens of thousands of people throughout the World. It is a sustained "on going" attack, and as always, ordinary people are in the firing line.

This is a time for cool heads.

My faith is as always, extraordinarily strong. If this is the end of time or Armageddon, I hope that we all do not suffer.

My angels continue to send signs in "numbers" and dreams. My writing continues, but why am I now writing about Lazarus and The Second Coming again?

Wednesday, 18th March 2020. Today, two years to the day after having major open-heart surgery I am returning to Leeds General Infirmary for an "echo" cardiogram at The Cardiac Investigation Unit in the Jubilee Wing. I am having a "sounding."

I have returned half a dozen times for appointments with my consultant, today is no exception.

This is my "spiritual" home.

Thursday, 19th March 2020. My recent visit to Cardiology for my echo cardiogram has left me with a strange feeling. It happened the whole time I was there, and it has spilled over into today. It is strange, but my feeling was one of upset, pain and anxiety. I have never felt like that before.

After taking time to ponder the situation, the outcome of it all seems to be down to the feelings of my "spiritual guide."

It was as if it was saying "why are you back here... why am I here?"

I had never felt like this before, it was as if it could feel everything that was going on there.

As the day progressed, I felt at ease, but the experience of yesterday will linger for a long time. I will have to return to Cardiology again, in the future, as they need to watch my condition.

I may find other feelings, as this is part of who I am now. It is as if I have a *dual* personality.

This can be the only rational explanation for my feelings.

Friday, 2nd February 2020. Approximately 1:13 a.m. In a dream...

It was as if I was in a cave. It had an area where the light came in. Children were in there too. Suddenly a voice said... "A leper grows at the side of thee (meaning angel Tom) then starts putting a knife through to kill the children. I picked up a large gold crucifix with my right hand, the light captured it and reflected outside on the murderer.

I remember distinctly shouting and saying in my sleep…

"The Lord is with me. The Lord protects me."

I then awoke in a daze.

Messages in numbers continue.

Friday, 27th March 2020. Approximately 9:22 a.m.

I found a "white feather" underneath our table in the dining room.

"Feathers appear when Angels are near."

Friday, 27th March 2020. Coronavirus update. We must self-isolate for three months, till the end of June. Never in all my days has anything like this ever happened before.

I have also completed my thirty-third drama out of my coma.

The name I have given to it is… "Why do you seek the Living amongst the Dead?"

The drama is in four parts and tells the story of a modern-day Lazarus and what happens to affect the future of humanity.

Lazarus, a citizen of Bethany, was resurrected by Jesus from the dead and brought back to life four days after his death over 2,000 years ago. The fulfilment of prophecy and a miracle.

Pontius Pilate crucified Jesus on the cross. Jesus rose from the dead three days after His death. The Resurrection of The King of Kings and The Messiah.

Now in 2020 a modern-day Lazarus, proclaims to be

from God.

Is this a myth or a prominent miracle?

As all of Italy is in complete lockdown due to the deadly Coronavirus the Vatican appoints Professor "Max" Brookstein to investigate and solve the mystery.

With Vatican State in lockdown... Monsignor Kevin O'Flaherty must work behind closed doors to help The Professor as The Holy See comes to terms with the modern-day plague.

Europe is now the epicentre of the virus.

A Global Emergency and Pandemic is now a reality.

Is all of this and the Lazarus claim part of what could be... The Second Coming... and the end of the World?

Strong stuff for someone who has never written until now.

Where does it all come from?

I have had several "complimentary reviews" for my writing and scripts for TV.

What TV Production Companies are saying.

"It sounds like you have had an extraordinary experience." (London Production Company)

"Thank you for sharing your story with us. It is always inspiring to read how people's experiences can bring about extraordinary change." (Leeds Production Company)

"What a remarkable story. The only way is up. We look forward to reviewing your work." (Liverpool Production Company)

I have also had reviews for my TV scripts and dramas.

ANGELS' EYES—BETWEEN THE LIVING AND THE DEAD (MAY 2020)

"I have just finished reading your script for Angels' Eyes. It is fascinating reading your story about how you have developed this love for writing since your coma. I hope you are in good health now. It is fantastic that you are writing so much, so many writers could only dream of the productivity you have so definitely keep it up."

"I think you have got an exciting opening to the episode with Rebecca saving the woman at the train station, potentially revealing her identity to the public. The whole premise of the show is remarkably interesting. There is also a great deal of humour to be there with these slightly out of touch angels returning to earth. There are funny lines throughout—I loved the "crying Mary" statue being caused by a "rusty pipe" and then the Monsignor saying that the rusting had been an act of God. I also really liked your sections with the angels not understanding modern music and people calling each other "love."

"You might want to think about adding more conflict to your story. There is conflict about the angels worrying about exposure by the public, but I think there needs to be more. For instance, when John Paul solves the "ghostly centurion" problem at the museum. He needs to command the situation more. What needs to happen is to create more drama and don't allow your characters to get away with it too easy. Overall, an exceptionally good drama." (Liverpool Production Company)

SKY HIGH—THE BEGINNING (REVIEWED AUGUST

2020)

"Thank you so much for sending us your script Sky High. I think you have picked a good setting. People love watching dramas set on the Riviera and a good old-fashioned spy drama would work well there, I think."

"You have an extremely dramatic opening to the episode, which is great. I would try to get to the action, after this scene, a little quicker. We seem to start with a lot of characters being briefed and introduced when you need to get flying into the show."

"I really like The Countess as a character, she could be very intriguing. It's quite exciting to have this quite "elegant lady" who is happy to roll her sleeves up and get involved with the other agents."

"I loved Steve McBride, as a character. I can imagine the audience loving him, even though he is a bit of a rogue."

"One bit of advice I would give you is for you to keep your scenes tight and leave the audience wanting more."

"Thank you again for sending Sky High. It was a joy to read." (Liverpool Production Company)

SINGLED OUT—A WORD IN YOUR SHELL LIKE (REVIEWED DECEMBER 2020)

"It was a very funny script from beginning to end. I would recommend that you need to prioritise plot over funny lines. It is quite common, among new comedy writers, for this to happen. Now you have tons of funny lines, which is great, but I do not think the story is not yet clear enough or strong enough at present."

"In general, a comedy should have a tight plot which

the jokes can hang off."

"You were right it is a remarkably interesting premise. I loved hearing about Zodiac and the club scene. I do think there is something interesting in watching something like that, in contrast to the more impersonal online dating. I really liked that we could tell there was some secret lurking under the surface for Gez, that worked nicely."
(Liverpool Production Company)

Excellent comments and advice, especially as I had never written for tv before, until three years ago.

Signs in numbers continue throughout the month.

Monday, 30th March 2020. My script for "Sky High!" is now on my laptop, with 6,333 words for my opening episode... The Beginning.

Tuesday, 31st March 2020. Today, I have emailed my TV scripts for "Sky High!" to ITV, and "Get Brexit Done" to the BBC. Another part of my ongoing story fulfilled.

Tuesday, 7th April 2020. I now have three dramas out for approval. It's tedious awaiting the outcome, and a wild guess, as there are so many who are in the same boat.

I confirm that I would never have done any of this had it not been for the "Gift" in my coma!

More signs in numbers begin to appear.

Friday, 10th April 2020. Good Friday.
No mass today—anywhere! The Coronavirus

pandemic is still highly dangerous and deadly. We are still in lockdown in the UK, there is no end in sight. Just over 980 people have died in England. The Doctors class me as "most vulnerable" due to my ongoing condition. All our lives are effectively *on hold* and we are all in the same boat.

I saw another "white feather" floating down when I opened the front door to go into the garage.

I end the month with yet more signs. Is this the "new way" of contact and perhaps a sign of what is to come?

Tuesday,28th April 2020. Time of 11:11 a.m. on Laptop.

1111 means you are "one with life" and with "all that is."

It is a signal that you should "live in the light that surrounds you" and experience a relationship with the Divine. It is also a sign that your past, present and future are converging, coming together.

Messages in numbers continue throughout May.

Tuesday, 26th May 2020. I spoke to my consultant on a phone call appointment. He said that my echo cardiogram was excellent. I may need to have an MRI scan in four months so they can "look at the aorta valve from another angle" but it was exceptionally good news indeed.

Thank you, God, Archangel Gabriel and especially to my Mum... she was right again.

When I visited the clairvoyant, she advised me that my Mum "was all around me."

As I write, we are all still in lockdown across the UK.

The economy has ground to a halt and a Worldwide recession is under way. Yet life must continue. I am doing my best in the twelve-week isolation period and taking care of my underlying problems.

If someone had told me in April 2018 that just over two years later, in May 2020 that I would have written thirty-seven TV series to date of TV dramas and seven books, all out of my coma I would have thought they were pulling my leg, but it's all true.

I have written seventeen series of "The Vatican Monsignor" to date, they are all in four parts. The following stories being part of the series are as follows... Crucifixion — Stigmata — Lazarus — The Saviours Coming. There is no end in sight.

How do you stop the "unstoppable?"

Messages still come in my dreams. When they do, they are incredibly significant, but most are in *numbers* daily.

God has answered all my prayers.

BEING AFFECTED

My writing now exceeds thirty-eight series.

I have written thousands of words. Simply put, it's non-stop.

My style of writing has changed and developed so much throughout the first couple of years and the numerical signs continue daily tying in with my current situation.

One day all of this will come together, although I know, I am on a journey of a kind... it's all part of "The Gift"—which continues to grow in strength.

June 2020. We are all in the grip of the Coronavirus pandemic. These are unprecedented times. We have never experienced anything like it in the World. We are still in lockdown in the UK although restrictions have now been removed by the government.

So many people have died. I am "shielding" and only partake in a daily walk near home or go to the local hospital for my regular warfarin check. The whole World is affected by Covid-19. Conspiracy theories continue to flourish. They are rife at present.

Wednesday, 3rd June 2020. Approximately 5:45 a.m. In a dream...

It was a song *playing* in my head... It was about dreams... It was being sang repeatedly. What does it mean?

Numbers continue as "signs" throughout June.

Monday, 29th June 2020. Approximately 4:20 p.m. In a

dream...

I had dozed off in an afternoon nap... I was back at my old house with my Mum and Dad and in the kitchen. I was about twelve years old. Someone was shaking the door hard and eventually they entered. It was a young woman. I was not sure who they were. She was a brown-haired person of medium build.

I asked, "where's my Mum?"

They replied, "she is in the park."

I said, "she's always in the park these days."

My Mum suddenly appeared near the rose trestling...

At that moment, my mobile phone went off with a message to update at exactly 4:25 a.m.

It was another reminder that my Mum is "all around me."

It all felt very real. I felt her presence.

Monday, 29th June 2020. Time on bedroom clock 4:44 p.m.

This is also in relation to the above dream; it is all very spooky...

444 is a sign someone is trying to communicate with you. It is also a sign that you are following the right path. If you see 444 repeatedly it is often your Guardian Angel giving you a sign that they are with you. The sign is reminding you to feel confident and supported in everything you do.

According to The Bible 444 is also associated with the ministry of Jesus. His ministry lasted 444 days until the moment Jesus is crucified.

Numbers in signs continue throughout June and into

July.

Sunday, 19th July 2020. Approximately 2:22 a.m. In a dream…

At a hospital. Looking into the future? Someone was charting what had happened in my life and in my coma. Someone I knew, as a boy, said they had an "all seeing eye." They started to talk about all I had done in my life, as if it were to repeat, all over again. They also talked about life after my coma.

More signs in numbers appear until the end of July and into August.

Wednesday, 5th August 2020. Approximately 5:45 p.m. In a dream…

I came out of an office and bumped into my sister. She was wearing a yellow striped dress. We hugged.

I asked, "what is it like where you are?"

She replied, "it's wonderful" and "do I want to know anything else?"

I asked, "how are my Mum and Dad?"

She said, "they are both ok."

My sister looked young and healthy.

My Dad died in 1980. My Mum died in 1987. My sister died in 2018.

Thursday, 30th August 2020. Approximately 1:30 a.m. In another dream…

A German Officer was cutting my neck…

I spoke these words, "the blood of The Hebrew God."

Further messages continue throughout September.

WHY DOES GOD SPEAK TO US THROUGH NUMBERS?

God speaks quietly through numbers; they are a Biblical means of how He speaks to his people. For those sensitive to "see" with prophetic vision, what God is revealing, they can hear His words through numbers.

Back in April 2020 I decided to write an updated version of an old '70s classic series...

"The Protectors 2020—Reborn for a New Generation."—This is how I wrote it...

International crime fighting agency based in London, Rome, and Paris.

Specialists in fraud, kidnapping and international intrigue. Harry Rule (Leader) based in London... Contessa Caroline di Conte (based in Rome), Paul Buchet (based in Paris).

Three private international detectives/trouble-shooters protect all who need their help. They belong to a Worldwide organization called – THE PROTECTORS.

When not working with Harry, Contessa runs her own detective agency which specialises in exposing art frauds and recovery of stolen art. Paul Buchet, works out of Paris... his is the researcher and gadget specialist.

New field Protectors... Miles Kingston and Shani Morgan work alongside Harry in London.

Can they help protect the World from all who pervert the course of justice... as the ultimate Protectors?

I followed this at the end of April, with an extremely unusual four-part series...

"GABRIEL—THE ARCHANGEL"— This is how I decided to write the series...

In December 2014 I had a dream and out of that I heard the words "The Book of Revelation."

Archangel Gabriel is known as "the Angel of Revelation" or announcement. He plays a significant role in Christianity... acting as the Messenger of God.

When the Vatican is made aware of a significant shift of values in Jerusalem, they assign Monsignor Kevin O'Flaherty and Professor "Max" Brookstein to investigate.

Catholic beliefs are under scrutiny. They try to obtain the facts and truth—what they find is a Revelation to the World.

In September 2017 in another dream... a young girl and her mother ask ... "who do you think you are?" A voice responds...

"WONDERFUL COUNSELLOR... I AM HIS MESSENGER."

To find the answer, and solution, someone claims to have seen Gabriel in a modern-day setting... but in truth, is it all a hoax or something amazing... and what bearing does it have on the World today?

This became my thirty-third series out of "My Gift."

In contrast, I followed that up with another four-part series called "Crucifixion."

My mind seemed to go into overdrive. I have never, ever written anything like this before. In fact, all my stories are different and never fail to amaze me. Again, "it beggar's belief," asking the question... am I writing this... or is it someone else?

"Crucifixion"—This is what I wrote as a synopsis...

The Romans pioneered a type of torture which became an ultra-efficient method of execution; the types of crucifixion varied around the Roman Empire. It was, and still is barbaric... they even had their own style of doing it.

Crucifixion is a type of punishment in which the victim is tied or nailed to a large wooden cross and left to hang, for several days, until dead.

The crucifixion of Jesus took place in Judea... between AD30 and AD33. Jesus became a threat to the stability of The Roman Empire and the power and might of Rome.

When a modern-day crucifixion takes place at a Passion Play in Oberammergau, Germany with tragic consequences, The Vatican sends Monsignor Kevin O'Flaherty and Professor "Max" Brookstein to investigate.

Was this an event that just went wrong or is it a cover up... and just who is the mysterious cloaked figure that appears at all the gatherings?

Is this a sign of ... The Second Coming?

Messages continue numerically throughout September.

Tuesday, 29th September 2020. Approximately 5:00 a.m. In a dream...

A child's bed at the bottom of the stairs. I climbed the stairs to find Jesus in bed. I knew it was Jesus because I saw the nail holes in His feet. I cannot remember if He spoke. We seemed to be on the coast and confusion reigned, as no one knew who he really was, then, I saw Jesus flying.

Friday, 16th October 2020. Approximately 9:00 a.m. A thought came into my head…

"Vanities of vanities… all is vanity."

Hebrew words translated into "vanity," Holy of Holies, King of Kings, God of Gods, Lord of Lords… the Hebrew way of maximising a word.

What does it all mean?

A CHANGE OF DIRECTION

A good friend pointed me in the right direction, for my next project. I had never heard of "The Georgia Guidestones" before, until he told me about them. The Guidestones are real.

It gave me an idea for my next Vatican Monsignor drama...

"The Georgia Guidestones"—This is how the story and synopsis read...

When a monument appears in Elbert County, Georgia in the United States of America it's almost identical to Stone Henge, but unlike its namesake the stones are not ancient but recent.

They carry controversial inscriptions in eight languages. While some people feel the messages in the inscriptions unite us, others feel they divide us.

Where did they come from and how did they get there?

When The Vatican hears of the recent findings, they send in Monsignor Kevin O'Flaherty and Professor "Max" Brookstein to investigate.

Is an unknown religious sect or movement behind it?

Are the messages a dangerous warning or conspiracy theory?

Why is the American government keen to cover up recent events?

Are the inscriptions foretelling the future?

When a vision in white appears by the stones and delivers a message, the World must decide if it is a warning or the end of time as we know it?

It was a complete departure from my earlier work. It opened the possibility of other areas for drama. My story took me in different directions through the course of my writing.

The "gift" out of my coma was again evolving and I too, along with it.

Visual messages in numbers continued in October and November 2020.

Whilst cleaning a mirror, a card fell to the ground… it read…

The Jubilee Year of Mercy

Thursday, 26th November 2020. Approximately 5:30 p.m. Paranormal activity in our dining room. The bulb in the lamp was *constantly* flashing as if things were passing through it.

Friday, 27th November 2020. Approximately 7:11 p.m. Paranormal activity going through left light in cooker hood in kitchen.

This continued again, on 28th November, it was all very unreal. The same thing happened on the 29th and 30th. Paranormal activity was rife then.

It started again on 1st December.

Wednesday, 2nd December 2020. Approximately 3:10 a.m. The Prayer for The Holy Souls… fell face down on to the carpet in the bedroom, just as it had done on 20th November.

Messages continue *in numbers* throughout December.

Thursday, 17th December 2020. Approximately 3:33 a.m. to 6:00 a.m. In a dream...

A huge cross in the sky with a plaque in white...

INRI... Jesus of Nazareth, King of the Jews

Then a figure of God appeared reaching down talking to the people below. I was with someone and approached the "vision."

THE END OF THE WORLD seeing a Cross in the Sky as a MESSAGE FROM GOD.

Tuesday, 22nd December 2020. Approximately 7:30 a.m.

The Christmas Star, The Bethlehem Star, The Great Conjunction... in the sky to the East. Sunrise below.

"There's a star in the east on Christmas morn."

The first time in eight hundred years and 2,000 years ago.

This is no coincidence.

Further messages in "numbers" continue in December.

Monday, 4th January 2021. We have a government update concerning the continuing Coronavirus...

All England is now in Tier 5 from Midnight. Yorkshire is currently in Tier 3. Death rates are increasing... infections are increasing. The Government classes it as an EXTREME EVENT.

The Government asks everyone to "shield" until mid-February.

Sunday, 10ᵗʰ January 2021. Approximately 11:53 p.m. In a dream…

A shining star/cross in a rail of clothes outside a shop and a well-known pop song playing.

No explanation.

WISE WORDS—"He that hears my word, and believes in Him who sent me, will have everlasting life, and shall not be condemned but will pass from death into life."

Back in November 2020 I also wrote a series called **"Predictions—Timeline." It was in four parts and dealt with the following…**

Nostradamus forecast ten predictions for 2020 with shocking expectations.

Are they all about to come true?

When the Pacific Tsunami Warning Centre in Ewa Beach, Hawaii issues a national emergency threat for a potential hit, The President takes control.

The Pacific Ocean is under constant levels of alert.

As the warning rises to LEVEL 4 an ice tsunami hits New York plunging the whole World into a disastrous timeline of fear.

When deadly earthquakes hit Italy the Vatican assign Monsignor Kevin O'Flaherty and Professor "Max" Brookstein to investigate.

Nostradamus predictions come true when a chilling prophecy and warning of a great plague begins in China and rapidly causes panic and disease on a Worldwide scale.

Can World Governments do anything to stop the ongoing life threating pandemic known as COVID-19?

How do you stop an unseen enemy?

Signs and messages in numbers continue throughout January.

Monday, 25th January 2021. Approximately 5:00 a.m. In a dream...
A Doctor who lives next door came to see me asking if I was ok.
I asked, "did my Mum send you?"
He said, "Yes... she wanted to know if you were alright?"

Wednesday, 27th January 2021. The coronavirus has now claimed over 100,000 lives in England. There are new variants that can spread from human to human.
These are worrying times.
Everyone must be careful. The government say that "darker days" may have come. Never, in my lifetime, has the World been under such a threat from an unseen enemy.

My writing for TV ventured into comedy drama towards the back end of January; I decided to draft a story set around "Batley Variety Club."

"Batley Variety Club"—The story is as follows...
Jimmy Corrigan had a vision to put Batley on the map in 1967 opening a Las Vegas style venue... that dream, and vision became known as the World famous... BATLEY VARIETY CLUB.

During its heyday, the club staged concerts by dozens of now well-loved entertainers. It was ahead of its time. It was the place everyone wanted to play. At its peak BATLEY VARIETY CLUB had over 300,000 members.

The club closed in 1978 but its legendary status lives on.

In this series of six heart-warming stories, we recreate the sights and sounds of the Seventies and the people whose lives it touched.

If you were there… if you were part of BATLEY VARIETY CLUB's amazing success… this one is for you—wonderful memories to share and cherish… relive BATLEY VARIETY CLUB… all over again.

WHERE THE WORLD'S TOP STARS PLAY

I drafted my "story lines" and decided rather than basing it on one central figure, I would take it in another direction. I wrote six completely different stories, then brought them all together in the finale.

My change in direction gave a new meaning to my stories. Memories of BATLEY VARIETY CLUB became extremely vivid.

It worked out to be very enjoyable and realistic. I had been countless times to the famous venue in the Seventies and my experience of it helped in my story lines. I was also born and bred in Batley, which is my hometown.

I remember "opening night" Easter Sunday, 1967. I was at college in Bradford then, and too young to go. It became a much-visited venue and was extremely popular with performing artists. People came from everywhere to the Variety Club.

I remember one afternoon, going to collect tickets for an artist in the Seventies. The receptionist on the foyer brought out the seating area plans. Suddenly a voice asks,

"Are you coming to see me flower?" I looked around to see, Charlie Williams, who at the time was a famous Yorkshire comedian from Barnsley. He had a "gift" for telling comical tales in his warm Yorkshire accent. Everyone loved Charlie.

I replied, "of course Charlie, who else" he laughed.

... but I was booking to see someone else.

The much larger arena venues of today, have all come out of that genre.

When I tell friends or people I have met about "my coma" experience and the "Gift" I received out of it, they are always amazed by my story. The fact is most people have never been in comas. I was like everyone else, until the day it changed my life. When you are in a coma you are on the precipice of life and death. You may not know it, at the time, but when they take you into the operating theatre there is a strong possibility that you may die on that table, as well as live.

You have a 50/50 chance of survival, not knowing which way it may go. All you can do is hope that you will survive the ordeal and be able to tell your story, if you have one, when you come round.

My story may be, quite extraordinary. I do not know of another one like it especially with regards to the "Gift" of being able to draft incredible stories, all of which, I could never have done in the years before it happened.

My signs in "numbers" continue throughout the month.

This is He, of whom it is written. Behold, I send my messenger before thee. They will prepare the way before you. LUKE 7:27

Friday, 12th February 2021. I have had my first "Pfizer" Covid vaccination. There are possible "side effects" as it is with all medicines.

My next project titled "The Language of Life" is in four episodes. I wrote it in ten days, mid-February.

I always feel, as if "my Gift" is taking me into areas I have never been. Sometimes I just don't understand why or the logic of it. Is it trying to teach me or tell me something?

My drama charts probably "unknown" things that have never been written before.

"The Language of Life"—This is my story...Secrets of our past, and revelations of our future, in the Book of Genesis link to all human genetic code.

We are all linked by a "hidden code" within our DNA often referred to as God's divine work or... The God Code.

The language of life.

A coded message has been found within human molecules deep within our DNA in each cell of our bodies. This is regardless of race, religion, heritage or lifestyle, and the messages are the same in every man, woman, and child, past and present.

When Professor Robert Kellerman and other scientists start all new, fascinating research, the eyes of the World are watching.

In Rome, The Vatican await results of the encrypted code messages and their translation.

Throughout history others have tried to find hidden or coded messages within The Bible's text.

Will the DNA discovery finally prove its existence?

To find the truth, Monsignor Kevin O'Flaherty works alongside, Professor "Max" Brookstein, but in doing so becomes caught up in a conspiracy concerning an "unknown power" and The Arc of The Covenant.

If all my dramas were developed for TV or film, I feel they would call for a distinct feeling of thrill and excitement. Throughout all my writing "my Gift" appears to be "satisfied" with what I have written. I do feel that I am being taken into certain stories and events, it is not by coincidence.

Numbers in "signs" continue throughout March.

Thursday, 25th **March 2021.** Approximately 9:38 p.m. Massive power surge in bedroom. It turned our TV off and the bedroom light blew. I also checked the fuse; this had blown too. The TV came back on 30 seconds, later flashing. It had moved three digital channels.

WHO ARE YOU?

EVER CHANGING STORIES

The "Gift" out of my coma seems to be always changing and adapting to different "untold" stories.

I know, it is a strange thing to say, but this is how it is. If I continue to write the way I do, am in control, or are they in control?

How long will it all last?

Your guess is as good as mine. There is no end in sight.

Whoever they are, they are powerful, more powerful than I could ever be. This is no illusion or dream. It is all true and real. There is no stopping this juggernaut. All I can do, is accept, that what has happened is "very special" and I continue to grow with it.

The next story, number fifty-eight.

"Shrouded in Secrecy" is about a subject I know nothing about...

Monsignor Kevin O'Flaherty is Head of Investigations at The Vatican under the watchful eye of Cardinal Raphael and His Holiness the Pope —Supreme Pontiff of Rome.

A secret organisation dating back about 7,000 years is at the centre of the investigation. The organisation was founded by the priests of Egypt, with the aim of preserving and protecting, all knowledge, past and present.

Top Secret documents are found in Rome, after a murder has been committed. The perpetrator takes refuge at The Vatican proclaiming his innocence and to be a member.

What The Monsignor must find out is the truth, which leads him into territory concerning a secret organisation.

A Vatican Intelligence Officer confirms a list in the hierarchy of the Catholic Church which shows evidence of a "cover up."

Cardinal Raphael asks the Monsignor and Professor Brookstein to secretly investigate. What they find could prove to be a "revelation" and a dangerous conspiracy founded to destroy the very heart of the Catholic faith.

Just where do you start with such a story?

I cannot believe that I have written about that, or any of the other stories, but I have, they have all been completed.

I am always amazed when the story starts to take shape. If I am "backed into a corner" I throw in something quite unexpected, for example, the storming of a US Embassy or different location, the Bahamas, or the Polar icecap. Nothing is impossible.

My only wish is to get to the end of the story, then it is on to the next one.

I decided to follow that story with another comedy drama in six parts called "SHEFFIELD FIESTA".

This picks up where BATLEY VARIETY CLUB left off.

I wrote this towards the end of March and completed it in mid-April.

"SHEFFIELD FIESTA"—My story is as follows...

A big, bold nightclub opened in 1970; its owners reputed it to be the largest in Europe and it was known as the SHEFFIELD FIESTA. Sheffield was a city with a booming industrial economy and high employment but by the 1980s the steel and coal industries went into steep decline.

The venue was lavish and had feel-good, old-fashioned entertainment with a stage, tinselly curtains, musical heroes, cabaret acts, and "chicken in a basket" served to dimly lit tables. It had resident, Fiesta Fawns, and waiter service. The Fiesta formula was an enormous success.

In this follow up to BATLEY VARIETY CLUB, this six-part comedy drama takes in various stories associated with SHEFFIELD FIESTA and the people who met or fell in love at the famous venue.

Now over fifty years later, I can tell the story of THE SHEFFIELD FIESTA. It was a joy to write. I had the same feeling when I wrote about BATLEY VARIETY CLUB.

I began with certain characters and stories which I weaved together. I finally brought them all together in the finale when the famous venue closed for the last time.

I remember going to see Mike Read, the comedian, in the mid Seventies. It was a "company night out" and the only time I visited the Fiesta. It left an impression and memories of a bygone age.

I am so glad that I captured the atmosphere in both comedy dramas —a time when variety was king. They have become personal favourites with regards my stories.

Messages continue in "signs" and numbers throughout March and April and into May.

Monday, 17th May 2021. Approximately 5:30 a.m. In a dream…

I could see angels coming towards me in the sky. As they became clearer and drew near, people were looking up. They did not know it was—THE END OF THE WORLD

In mid-April I decided to change direction with THE VATICAN MONSIGNOR. My next story in the series I called "LIFE SUPPORT." I wrote it in four parts.

"LIFE SUPPORT"—This is my story...

An alarming situation begins to unfold, when The Monsignor takes the train from Rome to Nice to meet Professor "Max" Brookstein for a NATO summit.

A young woman on board the train is assaulted. Luckily, the Monsignor is on hand to help, having trained as a boxer in Ireland. He stops the attack but falls after a surprise blow to the head.

The Monsignor is flown by air ambulance to a Catholic hospital by order of Cardinal Raphael. Doctors decide to put him into a deep coma and on "life support."

People in comas and on life support are "between Worlds," and you as their living family and friends are, in a sense, between Worlds with them. There are reasons why people linger in these "in between" states, one of them being, they do not cross over to the other side, because something is not finished.

Doctors say that The Monsignor's condition is, considered to be dangerous and "life threatening" as he is not responding.

Can "Max" awaken him from his deadly slumber and why are the attackers still in pursuit?

This story resonates with my own experience of being

"in a coma."

You go through every emotion. It is true when it refers to "being between Worlds" that is exactly how it was. It is an experience that you are never, ever likely to forget.

It became obvious to me, that some things are still unfinished and need to be finalised.

The "Gift" out of my coma is leading to something and somewhere incredibly special. I feel that my life has changed. I am different to the person I was before.

I am going forward. Where it will lead me is still unknown, all I know is that it is an incredible journey.

Tuesday, 25th May 2021. Approximately 19:05 p.m. Two light cream collared doves visit our birdbath.

A dove is a "symbol" of wisdom that may come in your life. There is no doubt seeing this is immensely powerful. If you see a pair of doves in front of you, or in a dream, then this symbolism will be even more powerful.

Numbers and signs continue throughout May and June.

Being of Irish descent, it was inevitable that one day, I would write something about Ireland. A famous Irish comedian used to say, "we Irish laugh at ourselves." I took that on board and decided to write a six-part comedy drama and it worked.

I tried various titles, eventually, deciding on "When Irish Eyes are Smiling". It was the perfect choice.

I did not have to wait long for inspiration to write my story. I decided I would go in the direction of "looking for my ancestral roots" and tracking down people that were still alive, and sure enough it began to take shape.

"When Irish Eyes are Smiling"—This is my story...

Gez has never been to Ireland.

When he discovers he is from a large family in Charlestown, County Mayo, he decides to make the journey from his hometown to search for his roots and ancestral heritage.

On arrival in Mayo, he makes the journey by bus to Charlestown, meeting the enigmatic Kathleen and finds out that both his Mum and Dad's parents originate from the same town.

When Gez finds unknown relatives on both sides, one being the Parish Priest—another being a rich American Irish Aunt, he must decide if he should remain loyal to his Yorkshire heritage or move to Mayo on a full-time basis.

He also finds CAIRN'S Bar on one side of the street and CULLEN'S Bar on the other.

When he enters one of the bars, he comes face to face with someone who looks exactly like him, even the Parish Priest has secrets.

With typical Irish comedy along the way—what could go wrong?

"When Irish Eyes are Smiling" has a wonderful mix of beautiful rural scenery, great storylines and characters that drive this gentle comedy drama, yet no one knows what is around the corner. "When Irish Eyes are Smiling" shows life can really be uncomplicated if you want it to be.

Be prepared to kiss the blarney stone...

I wrote this in February 2020.

It was a very satisfying project. I kept the comedy "low key," and everything fell into place rather well.

As you can see there is a certain amount of "mystery" and mischief about it. I suppose this can really happen if you go looking for someone in your past. The face-to-face situation was very funny indeed and the connection between the lead characters started to gel easily. There were various amounts of shenanigans going on. It was a pleasure to write. I felt a connection with my heritage.

It worked well, and of course I continued my writing.

For my next project, I thought I would write an "offbeat comedy drama." This was about "someone famous" and a "what if" scenario, if circumstances and fate had thrown two people together?

I decided this "chance meeting" would take place in Leeds, and out of it, my character, would go on to be a song lyricist and eventually a writer.

It sounds a bit like me...

It all came together extremely well. I also advised...

THIS DRAMA IS NOT REAL—BUT WHAT IF ALL OF THIS HAD REALLY HAPPENED?

What if... suddenly became a reality?

What if?

I based this on my own real "chance encounter" back in September 1976. I was at the Nouveau disco in Leeds, with a mate of mine... this is what happened...

We decided we would have another drink...

"Fancy a beer, Steve?"

"Yea, why not... two beers coming up."

We had just been in "Grobs" wine bar, a couple of doors down Eastgate. At that time, you could have up to two and a half pints before you hit the "legal limit."

I moved towards the bar. Suddenly this "skinny kid" came in, very slim, shock of black hair, grey bomber jacket. He pointed to the Bar lady, and she said tables were "reserved" in the restaurant.

What happened next was pure coincidence. We bumped into each other, and apologised, both of us laughing together.

It was a famous legendary pop star.

It is all true, it really is. I had tickets booked to see him at the Grand Theatre the next evening.

I never forgot that close encounter.

All of this is in my six-part story.

A friend also pointed me in the direction of another story. He told me about the "Antikythera mechanism" which was something I had never heard of before. I checked into the background and decided I would put pen to paper.

I tried two or three titles but decided to call it "The Antikythera Mechanism."

"The Antikythera Mechanism"—This is an idea of my story...

Divers find the World's first analogue computer below in a sunken Roman vessel in the waters of ancient Greece.

It is over 2,000 years old and discovered off the island of Antikythera.

The device used to predict astronomical positions and eclipses for calendar and astrological purposes decades in advance.

The ancient device is discovered stolen by staff at the

National Archaeological Museum in Athens. When NASA say that it has been turned on by the hand powered orrery, all the planets and moon align.

World Scientists advise of a pending major incident.

Cardinal Raphael assign Professor "Max" Brookstein and The Monsignor to investigate into the disappearance of the device by World Governments.

Can they stop it from changing the sequence of time before it is too late?

It was another complex story to write, but as usual, it was no obstacle for "My Gift." I wrote it in four parts within ten days.

In September 2020, I decided to write an updated version of a classic Sixties series. It also came under the banner of "Reborn for a New Generation."

My take was on an old Sixties TV series DEPARTMENT S. This is also in four parts, and I gave it the title of "Abandoned Loyalties."

In this series, it was a complete departure, from what I had previously written…

"Abandoned Loyalties"—This is an idea of what I wrote…

Department S are an elite branch within Interpol in Paris investigating international cases no one else can resolve.

Three super-efficient Agents head up the Specialist Section; Interpol Agents Alex Matthews, Robyn Davies and Mike McGowan head up the new team.

An International Bureaucrat is Head of Department S.

Their Chief instructs DEPARTMENT S to investigate by tracking terrorist networks across the World. Interpol insist on a "black out" to catch those involved in bringing them to justice.

DEPARTMENT S dispatch two Agents to East Sudan while Mike McGowan and Robyn Davies are sent to Hong Kong.

Alex and Annabelle find a plan in action to take over the World.

When DEPARTMENT S comes under threat Interpol must act fast to protect all concerned.

Later series have been written, all of which, I could not have written before in any form. I am always excited, when I have completed, yet another project. It feels, as if, my writing is going from strength to strength. My old method of writing story lines has changed. I do still feel this is helpful but in the main I, somehow, decide on a title, write the synopsis, and then draft my story around it.

It is a simple formula, but it works, and as I have said before, I write it quickly and with no writer's block.

I don't know of anyone else who has received "A Gift" like mine out of a coma.

Today I heard something quite distressing, heart-breaking news about a girl aged twenty-three who had only weeks to live due to cancer. There was also another girl of twenty-nine who had the same timescale to live.

There is nothing you can do. You can give no answer. There are no answers when this happens. My own sister died of cancer. The "Gift" out of my coma predicted the future. I didn't know what it meant, at the time, but it saw this coming.

I thought "the coffin" in the room was for me, it turned out not to be for me at all.

The power of prayer is powerful. God hears our prayers.

I know someone, somewhere, heard my prayers, and sent me messages of comfort, at a time when I needed it. God has worked wonders for me, and my life is in his Hands. I have great faith. It has always been a huge part of my life. It has sustained me through everything. I have had to make sacrifices and take different roads, even with family matters, but I have stuck to my faith through thick and thin.

I somehow know that everything I have been through was for a reason, and that one day I may reach what I am looking for.

Inspiration is everywhere.

After writing The Antikythera Mechanism I decided to follow it up with...

"Where Time Doesn't Exist"—I wrote this in January 2021.

Pompeii was an ancient city that suffered the volcanic eruption and devastating effects of Mount Vesuvius along with Herculaneum and dozens of Roman villas in AD79.

On the outskirts of Pompeii, a house known as "The Villa of Mysteries" holds a series of exquisite frescoes and a secret withheld from the outside World.

When Archaeologist's discover a modern-day fresco in

2020 depicting the end of the World in 2021, Governments go into meltdown.

Professor "Max" Brookstein and The Monsignor team up with Oxford Professor Robert Kellerman when a Roman time capsule is found by archaeologist's in a recent excavation—thousands of years old, at the villa.

In a place, where time stands still, and where there are no answers, will the ancient find reveal what is about to happen?

Will ancient Pompeii give up its secrets and is the World ready to find out?

Pompeii is without doubt, one of the most interesting places to visit. It attracts over 2.5 million visitors a year and it is a World Heritage site. I visited there with my partner. We were on tour, and this was a place, I had always wanted to visit. We didn't bother with the organised tours as it was virtually just one stop down on the train from where we were staying in Vico Equense.

However, we made a mistake of not having a tour guide, nor did we pick up a tour pamphlet before we started. I would say that it is one of the most incredible places I have ever visited. Thousands of priceless artefacts have remained intact. The tour happened six years ago before my relapse and operation.

The whole place had a strange feeling. You could feel a presence. I think it would come *alive* at night; it was that kind of place. I settled on my four-part drama, and it all came together quickly.

We may all be dying inside from the day we are born. There are hundreds of questions asked by people on this taboo subject. Even the mystery of, does life exist after we die, as in *everlasting* life? This is a question asked by many people.

As I have said before, all you need is faith to believe.

I am who I am, with all my flaws. I am not perfect. Only God is perfect.

Yet when Jesus chose His disciples, he chose ordinary men with no airs or graces, ordinary fishermen, a tax collector, and others to follow Him.

God has blessed me with the "Gifts" I have received.

WE ARE EACH GIVEN A GIFT.

This is what I wrote in 2016…

I don't think that I am special, with the "Gift" I received from God, as a "reader." I cannot predict or feel things in a certain way. God gives other visionaries talents to do this. There was a horrific murder in Birstall six years ago, when Jo Cox the local MP was murdered by a local man. I have passed the area where it took place and tried to get a *feeling,* but it didn't work—I felt nothing.

My role is completely different. I am unable to do anything there. I obviously feel the raw emotion like everyone else, but I am not able to do anything spiritually, it is not in my power to do so.

There are signs in lots of things, I am fortunate, being able to read them. Songs in particular, their titles or lyrics, books that I seem to stumble upon, they all mean something. We are all surrounded by things that can reach into our inner being. We may be more complex human beings than we know.

Answers are not easy to find. We can only surmise when something happens in our lives, it is for a reason.

There are no answers.

WHY ME? ... WHY WAS I CHOSEN?

There was a reason I didn't die. God gave me a second chance; I was within a hairs breath of death. I almost died, within distance of touching Heaven... Why? ... Why me?

It had to be for a reason, a purpose; I had to validate my life. It must be worth something, mean something... Why? ... Why me?

Are they warning signs from Heaven?

Messages spoken by Angels in dreams are real. You don't choose them... they choose you... Why? ... Why me?

Jesus said, "All who believe in me, whether they are living or dead, shall never die, but will live."

He also said, "I am the Way, the Life, and the Truth."

The Second Coming of the Christ... I wonder will we all be ready?

For my next project, I decided to write two series about a famous Oxford detective and they both worked out well. They don't come under the banner of "reborn series" but as stand out stories on their own.

My first series was in four parts called "Coded Messages—Divided Loyalties."

I tried to write it as complex as I could and in keeping with the original.

"Coded Messages—Divided Loyalties" This is my Story...

When coded messages are found at the murder, scene the detectives on the case are asked to crack mysterious ancient Egyptian inscriptions, after a series of murders in Oxford—by someone known as the Sphinx.

In this complex investigation the detectives must use all their ingenuity and passion to succeed by breaking hieroglyphic codes to track down the killer. Does the key to the murders have anything to do with the Institute of Criminology in Oxford and are they following a pattern? Why is an Oxford Don a prime suspect?

My follow up series was due to hearing two words on my TV. It was in an old Eighties series, the words spoken were "Sanctum Sanctorum."

When I checked, I saw that the meaning was "holiest of holies."

Another coincidence?

I logged the words and kept them for a series in the future.

I decided my next Oxford series would be titled "Sanctum Sanctorum."

"Sanctum Sanctorum"—This is an outline...

I used my famous detective again to solve the mystery.

When new forensic evidence appears, it links four unsolved murders in Oxford from over twenty years ago.

A young Oxford graduate, on her way home is found by walkers. She has been strangled near a canal. A cryptic crossword left at the scene is the only clue.

The Chief Constable drafts in senior detectives to solve the riddle and puzzle left by the murderer.

Can they solve it in time, before more murders are

committed?

I have to say, there is no sex whatsoever, in any of my writing, swear words are taboo too.

I have written everything straight from the heart, with key locations and details provided by the Internet.

My stories are still original. Whenever I start to write something, I let the story take me where it leads me. There is no force majeure.

If for instance I begin in Rome, I may eventually decide to fly to New York or London. It really is that simple. As for the story, it seems to all come together, one way or another; I don't plan anything. Nothing is set in concrete. Everything is spontaneous.

After writing TV scripts about Batley Variety Club and Sheffield Fiesta, I decided to write a "family orientated" comedy drama for my next venture. I don't know how I came upon the idea, but I based it in Leeds, and it is centralised around a certain family.

It was yet another masterpiece that came straight out of "The Gift" in my coma.

I decided that it would have significant amounts of music. It is set in the '80s.

I based it on characters I have known and met during my lifetime. It all came together beautifully. It was another joy to write.

"Family Ties"—This is how the story goes...
Life's main ingredients are about all the things we put into it and what we get out of it.

Are we about to discover what really makes us happy?

Can we create our own recipe for happiness?

The Caine family in Leeds make up of Joe, (Dad) an industrious down to earth Yorkshireman of Irish descent.

Melanie, (Mum) is a nurse in the city and looks after three daughters —Rebecca, Laura, Samantha, and baby brother Brett.

Peter and Monica are the elderly grandparents and patriarchs of a bygone era.

Six feel good stories drive this comedy drama showing how people cope, no matter what life throws at them.

Set in the '80s with a soundtrack to match.

This could be any family, anywhere.

THE FEEL-GOOD FACTOR—IS BACK.

It was, surprisingly, an easy story to write. I decided to base my six story lines on matters we all encounter in our lives.

It was a complete departure, from all the other things I had written before, but it was still very satisfying. I decided to go full circle in this series, and everything turned out as I expected it to. I dealt with various family matters.

The subjects covered were as follows:

Creating your own path.

Being able to cope—no matter what happens.

Having a reason to smile—the best medicine.

Setting your own spirit free.

Following your own dreams.

I focused on old fashioned family values which added to the mixture in all my stories.

Where all of this comes from is still a mystery, and it

continues to show no sign of stopping!

It was another satisfying project.

It was in complete contrast to all the other series I had written. These are not "one off" stories, they are made up of 12,6,4 and 3 episodes each. Two or three series need more work than others, but it's a road I am happy to take.

It is now over three years since I had open-heart surgery at Leeds General Infirmary, and I thank God every day for saving my life.

Had I not had surgery, I would not be here today. Luckily, we live in an age, where technology has advanced. This is one of the good things that has come out of progress. It will only get better as we move forward in the future.

The vaccines for the coronavirus have been incredible. Hopefully, we may all be able to return to a normal life in the not-too-distant future. The sad part is that so many people have died. We have been advised that we will have to learn to live with coronavirus in future; it will always be there, one way or another. It will be part of all our lives in the coming years.

That is unless another incredible technological advancement is made. Who knows what will happen in the future?

In August 2020, I decided to involve The Vatican Monsignor in a completely different assignment. The story is called "Declassified" and it was written in four parts.

"Declassified"—This is the story outline...

Monsignor Kevin O'Flaherty is no ordinary priest. He loves the classics, has a taste for golf, and Guinness, all things Irish and has a nose for "solving the unknown."

The Monsignor is Head of Investigations at The Vatican under the watchful eye of Cardinal Raphael and His Holiness the Pope—Supreme Pontiff of Rome.

When a Roman Catholic Priest dies in mysterious circumstances, during a visit to a former establishment secret location, it opens a complex issue that leads to the very top of Government.

The Vatican assign The Monsignor and Professor "Max" Brookstein to investigate alongside Oxford Professor Robert Kellerman. They stumble on answers that will rock the World.

The secret location was the World's best kept secret and remained so until 1975, but when secrets of the past collide with the future The Monsignor and "Max" find themselves targets, in this cat and mouse conspiracy story.

Coded secrets may be the answer.

Will they find out why the victim died and who is behind possibly the World's notorious cover up of all time?

The Monsignor is rushed to hospital in Oxford where another "diplomatic incident" is about to take place.

This was a tricky but factual story. I never make it easy when I write any of my stories. In fact, I try to make them as difficult, and as complicated as possible. They involve certain twists and turns, to bring them to life. I live those characters and what they are going through; I would think that many writers will do the same to get to the finish line and ultimately, the end of the story.

I have made my "Monsignor" character out to be an Irish man with staunch values and beliefs. His love of the modern classics, golf and his native Ireland are all there in my stories.

His world is set within The Holy See at the Vatican. He is precise and meticulous. He has an *eye* for solving the complicated with perhaps a glint in his eye.

In my opening story, THE SAVIOUR'S COMING, he soon gets into hot water with Professor "Max" Brookstein when he arrives at JFK airport in New York...

"Hi, I'm Max."

"A woman?"

"How very perceptive of you, Monsignor."

"I thought Max was a man's name."

"It's short for Maxine."

"I'm sorry Max, forgive me?"

The Monsignor makes his apologies and he and "Max" go on to have a good working relationship and become exceptionally good friends.

It's essential to have central characters who drive the story, and "Max" and The Monsignor's continuing friendship supplies the human element to the series.

Of course, there are a couple of series, that I have just not written yet. The idea or title may come to me one way or another. They are logged into my storylines book waiting to be possibly written at some stage.

The ones that spring to mind are...

FAKE and MOVING HEAVEN

FAKE — is about an ever-changing World where only

two kinds of people succeed. Those who have everything and those who fake their way in life—to get everything.

This six-part drama will be set in London.

New Scotland Yard and MI6 work together to fake their way ahead of criminals, ultimately bringing them to justice.

MOVING HEAVEN — is a continuation of my own story of events and what happened before and after being in a coma.

Eventually, these stories will be written sometime in the future.

When I think of my next venture, I sometimes decide to go in the direction of writing *lighter* stories in between my staple diet of drama and comedy drama. This happened recently when I decided to write a musical type of drama for my 62nd series.

It was about a famous singer, and the first thirty years of their career.

I decided to write it in six parts of five-year segments. This would mean that if I were to write it up for a sixty-minute script, I could only devote twelve pages to each year. It would be a tall order, but nothing is impossible when it comes to "My Gift."

You can do anything if you set your mind to it!

I am aiming to conclude the next thirty years, later in the autumn. I expect this to be like its predecessor, and no doubt, quite as entertaining.

That is what it is all about when writing for TV; entertaining your audience, keeping them captivated with your story lines. Taking them on a journey.

Whatever happens you must write something that is

fresh and real. I call all my stories "fiction based on fact."

Maybe one of my stories, says it all. It is called "A Feeling of Déjà vu."

I wrote this in four parts in July 2020.

"A Feeling of Déjà vu"—This is the story outline...

We are all searching for answers to make the best of our lives. We all will have experienced a state of déjà vu at certain points in our lives while making our way in the World.

The phrase translates as "already seen" in a paranormal or precognition setting—prophecy may also be another feeling.

While on retreat in Oxford, Monsignor Kevin O'Flaherty meets Professor Robert Kellerman. He suffers a seizure and is diagnosed by doctors with having a mild form of epilepsy, which can be triggered by being in a state of déjà vu.

The Vatican becomes extremely concerned with The Monsignor's health and dispatch an Envoy to meet Professor Brookstein in Oxford.

Doctors also become concerned when The Monsignor slips in and out of a coma. Robert and Max must deduce a case concerning the Vatican in his absence.

Is this the end for The Vatican Monsignor?

Maybe we all have had a feeling of déjà vu in our lives, at one time or another. It can be triggered by experiencing something that we have already been associated with in our past.

I don't know what made me write this story. Maybe the words déjà vu has been the influence in a lot of my writing. It's hard to explain what really happens to make me think about certain things for my story lines. All I know is everything comes together; nothing is left to chance.

Numbers and signs continue to show me the way.

My life is still on a journey, maybe my writing is part of that, whatever's happening it has opened my eyes to everything.

It is incredible to think, that I have written so much. My stories all take different directions. I've written about earthquakes, solar eclipses, divine providence, and subtle illusions. My series have taken in the second wave of the coronavirus, divided loyalties, and conspiracy theories. I have combined them with various comedy drama's written in the '60s, '70s and '80s. I have written about things I have never heard of, the Antikythera mechanism and the Georgia Guidestones, they both exist but I didn't know it. The various series about Crucifixion, feelings of déjà vu, epicentres, coded messages, and The Saviour's Coming were a revelation. I also wrote about The Turin Shroud, Lazarus and the Ten plagues of Egypt, all in a modern-day setting.

I have taken my "Vatican Monsignor" character in various directions too. Never knowing whether he would continue as he was or may be end one way or another. Throughout it all the characters and story remain strong and positive. It's no good writing about negative things. A writer should be positive.

My "Gift" still shows the way.

I have written seventy-five series to date. I don't know how many more stories will come out of my coma. It could be a hundred, a thousand, who knows. All I know is that this incredible "Gift" has created all of them. If someone else "crossed over" with me, as my clairvoyant advises, maybe they are the ones responsible for all of this.

My Guardian Angel may hold all the answers.

In October 2020 I decided to write about "Devine Providence." It was in four parts and another in my Vatican Monsignor stories...

"The two most important days in your life are the day you are born and the day you find out why" Mark Twain.

The Eye of Providence or the all-seeing eye of God is a symbol meant to stand for divine intervention.

"Devine Providence"— This is an outline of my story...

When a set of ancient symbols are sent to The Vatican addressed for the Monsignor, they claim to have a meaning that the end of days is near—leading to an investigation which takes him in many directions in search of the truth.

As a second wave of Coronavirus grips all nations, governments believe this to be part of the prophesied Seven Seals of Judgement in the Book of Revelation.

Are the symbols linked to the end of the World?

The whole World is plunged into a timeline of fear.

Is the day coming when we all will find out why?

Can anything be done to stop the ongoing life-threatening pandemic known as COVID-19?

How do you stop an unseen enemy?

This was a very chilling drama to write. I could see

there would be hundreds of questions that came out of it.

Would we all see the end of the World and bear witness to the truth?

How can this happen in a modern-day World?

All my stories have come out of my coma; I am still coming to terms with what happened when I was in theatre for eight hours, on life support, not knowing if it was the end of everything.

As my own continuing story unfolds before me, I now accept, that my life was saved for a reason.

We all must get as much as we can out of life. Our lives are short, the unseen coronavirus, which is before us, has changed all our lives. My only wish is to continue the road I am on. I have a feeling that my writing will go on, possibly until I can write no more.

My story is true, real and it continues today.

My current drama is called "DEFCON" it is set in Taipei and the United States.

"DEFCON"—This is the story outline...

A secret stealth plane goes missing while on manoeuvres in the South China seas.

A task force is dispatched to look for the missing plane.

The President puts the country into DEFCON (The Defence Readiness Condition), at LEVEL 3.

It's a game of cat and mouse.

Will the weapon be found before World War 3 erupts?

This is yet another story out of my "Gift."

As I come to the end of "My Story" it is perhaps fitting

to say...

GOD WORKS IN MYSTERIOUS WAYS, HIS WONDERS TO PERFORM

Those were the very first words I wrote when I started to draft this book.

I have written six books to date, with another that links music to memories.

Numbers and signs continue to flourish, there is no end in sight.

Whoever it is, whoever they are, my guide and spiritual guide, seem to be beside me on my journey. They "light the way" before me. They are my "guiding light."

Everything I have said, everything that has been written in this book, is the truth.

God has given me the grace, to continue with my life.

I am a new man, after my life saving operation. My eyes have been opened. I seem to have taken on a new meaning, a new direction.

My only hope is that I continue to live a full life and that my "spiritual awakening" helps me to see everything in a new light.

Being in a coma and getting a wonderful "Gift" out of it was life changing. I hope my story will somehow change your life, and maybe through my words, you will come to know, that things can change under extreme circumstances.

People in comas are "between Worlds" and in a sense their friends and family are "between Worlds" with them; I think this best describes what it is like being in a coma.

In conclusion, I had a dream on Friday, 8th October

2021. Approximately 11:30 p.m. My Mum said, "Everything is real."

I replied, "I know it is."

This was quite significant, as I had not received a message like this for over three years.

Are they starting all over again?

It was again spoken at the point of waking. I remember waking up stunned and dazed, yet it was all very real. My Mum hadn't spoken to me since October 1987—thirty-four years ago. It was also the first time that I was able to respond telepathically. I don't know how or why this happened?

The last time my Mum spoke was when I saw a Clairvoyant for a reading in October 2018.

October is the month of the Rosary in the Catholic Church for devotion to the Blessed Virgin Mary. The liturgical feast of Our Lady of The Rosary is celebrated annually on October 7th.

I hope my story, has given you an insight into what happens before and after being in a coma.

Whether everyone gets a "Gift" out of being in a coma remains a mystery.

What we do in life echoes in eternity.

This was My Story. True and real.

It continues today.

ABOUT GERRY

Before embarking on writing my first book BETWEEN WORLDS: MY TRUE COMA STORY, I worked in various business roles for fifty years.

It was in my last role that my writing career developed. In the late eighties/early nineties I ran events for ITV TELETHON 90 and 92 with NEXUS and OASIS in Leeds. The highlight being having one of our events staged in the main arena at HAREWOOD HOUSE. Nexus awarded me Gold Card status for my achievements. There were only eight cards issued in the country. It was a prestigious award. My Events and shows were very entertaining and form part of my story.

After undergoing major open-heart surgery at LEEDS GENERAL INFIRMARY in March 2018, I received a "gift" out of my induced coma. So far, I have written seven books and seventy-five TV series to date. I had never written books or for TV prior to being in a coma.

I have decided to tell my true story to the World. I hope that through my words you will come to know that exceptional things can happen after being in a coma.

www.blossomspringpublishing.com

Printed in Great Britain
by Amazon